C000101612

SURVIVE AND THRIVE

*To the memory of my mother Peggy
and my grandmother Brigid*

CONTENTS

ACKNOWLEDGEMENTS

My heartfelt thanks to my husband Seán for his continued support and patience and to my eight children whom I love dearly. My thanks to my sister Miriam Owens for being there for me; to my dear friend Sheila Fitzgerald for her kind nature, integrity and honesty; and to Ruth and Mike Lambe for their support throughout many years; to my close neighbour Dawn Mason, who reminded me of many forgotten details of my childhood.

My deep gratitude to all my staff at ABC Cleaning Services and Supplies. Thank you to my investors and to all my loyal clients and customers.

I wish to acknowledge and thank the following: Peter McDermot for his professional guidance and advice; the Kerry Businesswomen's Network (KBN) for their loyalty over the years—they are a wonderful network of people; Margaret Brick, founder and editor of *Connect* magazine; Donna Kennedy, who I admire as an inspirational speaker and best-selling author; Pat Slattery, entrepreneur and business mentor, for his continued professional mentoring and support and for encouraging me to raise the bar to become the best I can be.

My gratitude to Bridget McAuliffe for her editing and publishing work and to Kieran Nolan for the artwork he created for this book. Thanks also to John Walsh Photography.

ACKNOWLEDGEMENTS

INTRODUCTION

IT HAS TAKEN much of my life journey to learn that life is not just about surviving, but also about thriving. There are times when all we can do is hang in there and survive, but that is not enough; we have to thrive in order to become the people we are capable of being. For many years, however, mere survival was my goal. I thought that if I could just get through the next twenty-four hours and manage to keep all the balls in the air, I'd be happy. Getting to the end of the day without a major disaster happening was my aim. If I achieved it, I'd go to bed relieved at having survived another busy and chaotic day while already dreading what challenges the next day was going to bring.

It has taken a long time—and many ups and downs, failures and successes—to learn that survival alone isn't enough; the truth is, if I wasn't thriving, if my family and business weren't thriving, then our lives were being lived at a level that was neither nourishing nor inspiring. To survive the challenges that life throws at us is vitally important, but to really flourish and grow our talents, and to move steadily towards the full expression of our goals— despite or because of the circumstances in which we find ourselves—is what thriving is about.

My early years were all about survival. I was born into rural poverty in a family where violence and excessive drinking dominated my childhood landscape and where eight of my nine siblings were put into care. My mother lived with the tragedy that TB brought to her younger years and which caused her great pain. She was exemplary in her efforts to care for her own growing family, against huge odds and without the support of her husband.

Survival was what those early years were all about and in that struggle I was lucky to find support in the love and protection that my grandmother gave me. I also survived by developing a very strong work ethic that gave me a sense of purpose; by focusing on giving to others when I cared for my siblings; and by creating an imaginary friend whom I could trust and who listened without prejudice to everything I told her.

All these elements helped me to survive the harshness of my upbringing but, even as a child, I instinctively knew that there had to be more to life. When I was fourteen, I was minding the most recent addition to the family (of which I was the eldest); I held her high over my head and declared to her uncomprehending ears, 'One day I will be my own boss. I will have my own business and house'.

It was several years later, when I was a young adult, before I experienced for the first time the joy that thriving brings. I had left school early to start working full time and, when I was sixteen, I met the man who became my soulmate and husband. Our shared love and the freedom to express it was a flourishing in my life where such expression was—at best—rare, or, more often than not, absent. Our new family life began in our shared dreams which soon became real as we set up home and had the first of our eight children.

Of course, it was never going to be easy and soon we were facing the daily trials that all young couples face. The disease of alcoholism, from which my husband suffered, was an added challenge and a difficult aspect in the fabric of our family life. There is no doubt that, some days, basic survival was again a goal that I was happy to reach. However, I never forgot my dream of creating a life that was better than the one I'd had growing up, where I could provide properly for myself and my family; a life where we had security and the space to grow and thrive. Setting up my own business was my way of following this dream.

Somehow, out of the challenges that my early life presented, I learned resilience, determination and self-belief, as well as developing a never-give-up attitude. These attributes served me well as I chartered the sometimes very choppy waters of starting and developing a business where each new day brought new lessons to be learned. I didn't come from a business background but, from the age of twelve, I worked for a successful business family and learned much in my time with them that has stood to me throughout my life.

From running a home-based shop to homebaking, cleaning buses, running a newsagent's and general shop, I had many stepping stones along the way to setting up

ABC Cleaning, a contract-cleaning company, the business that saw my long-term goal realised. While many of those early businesses were short-lived, I learned lessons from each and every one of them that I continue to value to this day.

The motto 'never give up' is hardwired into my brain and it has kept me going when it seemed there was nowhere left to go; when it seemed that we had, finally, reached the end of the road. This was almost the case during two national recessions when we came close to losing everything. But I was always determined to never give up; I believed that we could survive even when my endurance and our business were tested to the very limits.

I had to do things that I really didn't want to do—including finding an investor for the company when my back was to the wall—but I was not going to give up and reminded myself that half a loaf was better than none. We survived, and with sacrifice, endurance, being open to learning more lessons and—crucially—being able to ask for and accept support, we turned a corner and started to thrive again. ABC Cleaning is now in a good place and the future looks bright, though we don't take anything for granted.

I am an ordinary person who always wanted a life that was better than the one I was born into; I was a young mother who wanted to ensure that her children would have lives that were about more than mere day-to-day survival. I have worked very hard to make the dream of a thriving personal, family and business life become a reality. It has rarely been easy and the success I have achieved has been a long time coming.

In the course of my life journey, I've learned many lessons about surviving and thriving, both personally and in business. The key lessons that I've learned and that guide me each day are:

- No matter what your background is, what kind of upbringing you've had or what personal challenges you have, you can achieve what you want in life with self-belief, determination and hard work
- Learn from the mistakes you will inevitably make and move on from them
- Identify and draw on your strengths
- Avoid negative people who undermine positive energy
- Work at what you love
- Don't treat your days as a rehearsal for another day; no day comes around a second time
- Keep focused on the road ahead, not the road you've just travelled
- Be kind to yourself
- Do your best and remember that perfection doesn't exist
- Never give up on your dreams

I have always been a networker, a talker and a listener. I've loved listening to the stories of others and I've taken some nugget from every single story I've ever heard. When we listen, we learn. I believe that when we tell our story, we create an opportunity to support and help each other as we make our way along the road of life. In telling my story, I hope that you will learn from my experiences so that you, too, can not alone survive but also thrive.

Breeda Hurley, April 2017

CHAPTER ONE

EARLY FOUNDATIONS

BEFORE going into town to collect her pension on a Friday, my grandmother—or Nan, as we called her—would put on her finery. She loved getting dressed up and always went through the same ritual before her weekly visit to Tralee. On Thursday night she would spit on her shoes and rub them until they shone. Before leaving the house on Friday, she would carefully comb her hair—which she only washed once a year, on Christmas Day, in order to avoid getting a cold—and curl it using hair pins. She couldn't afford blusher so she would get some crepe paper that was left over from Christmas and rub it to her cheeks for a bit of colour. Finally, she'd put on her coat and gloves. Then Miss O'Neill, a neighbour, would collect her in her pony and trap and they'd head for town.

She loved her Friday outings. After she'd collected her pension she would do a bit of shopping at Nora Deady's in Moyderwell. There was a bar attached to the shop and Nan would repair into the snug and have a glass or two of porter while chatting with the other women there. In 1950s and

1960s Ireland, it was frowned on for women to drink in the main bar or at the counter. She liked her little drop but Nan's real love was snuff. I can still remember her taking a pinch and saying, 'The Lord have mercy on the dead. It isn't the world we live in at all but the people that's in it'.

She often made homemade bread and you might get a bit of snuff in a slice even though she always washed her hands. You'd see the brown of the snuff, cut that part off and eat the rest. Christmas was important to her and she would decorate the house with holly and red crepe paper. She'd always make sure there was a goose for dinner which she'd cook on the open fire, setting the pot on the embers and putting the warm ashes on top of the cover so it was heated from above and below.

Nan had a very kind heart in spite of having to endure a hard, impoverished life. I knew that she loved me and I loved her back as much. Her name was Brigid and I was called after her and I think that added to our bond. She watched out for me and did her best even when times were tough, making sure I got whatever food was going, be it a boiled egg or a bowl of porridge. I not only loved Nan, I also respected her and always saw her as one of the best influences in my childhood. She was a woman who lived through tough times but she never gave up, no matter how challenging life got.

She was married three times, a bit of a record in those days when it was very hard to find even one man to marry unless you had a dowry of some kind. Nan didn't have money but she was a very good-looking woman, thin and small in stature. She was also a great worker and was employed by many farmers around the area before she got married. She also ran a little shop in Farmers' Bridge, a rural townland about three miles from Tralee.

Her first husband was Maurice O'Shaughnessy who came from a popular family of blacksmiths in the local area. They had a son and daughter but, sadly, Maurice got sick and died. Nan then married Dan Moriarty in 1919 and they had five sons, including Paddy (my father), Danny, Michael and Johnny; their other son, Tom, died when he was only five years old. Then Dan died prematurely and now there were six children without a father and only Nan to look after them. 'I reared a faction without a father,' she used to say. She had to put food on the table and so had no choice but to go back to work on farms in north Kerry. When she came home in the evening, she'd put on a pot of potatoes for the children. While she was out working they had to fend for themselves and, when they were hungry, they would call to the neighbours during the day in the hope of getting something to eat.

In 1940, Nan married for a third and final time. She was in her late fifties and her children were older when she met and married Paddy Sugrue. After their wedding, she left the little house with the shop and moved a short distance back the road to a house in Caherleaheen. Paddy had pensions from both the Irish and British Armies and Nan continued to get a small income from these after he died.

MY FATHER, Patrick (Paddy) Moriarty, was born in 1921, the second eldest in a family of five boys. From a very young age, he had a lot of responsibility on his shoulders as Nan was out from early morning until late in the evening, working to try and make ends meet. He left school at thirteen and began working as a farm labourer. His brother Michael went to England for a while but returned later and settled down in Tralee, while his brother Johnny lived with Nan all his life and also worked as a farm labourer. My father had a stepsister and stepbrother from Nan's first marriage. His stepbrother emigrated to England while his stepsister married locally and lived with her husband and children at Nan's until her husband died tragically following a railroad accident. After that, she and her family moved to Tralee town.

Danny, my father's eldest brother, went to England in the early 1930s when he was fourteen years old. He didn't keep in touch with the family and they had no idea what had become of him. Nan never forgot him and she always put a single flower in front of the statue of the Sacred Heart in the kitchen, praying that he was safe and that she would see him again. One stormy night, in 1957, he appeared at the front door. He'd joined the British Navy and the ship he was on had been caught in a very bad storm. They anchored at Fenit Harbour waiting for the storm to pass. Nan was over the moon to see her son for the first time in over twenty years. He only stayed the one night as his ship was leaving the next day. They never again met after that visit.

When Danny died in 1984, he was living on his own in a small flat somewhere in Liverpool. My father was contacted by police when he passed away and made the trip to Liverpool with my brother to identify his remains. In later years, Danny had worked in a place called Ben's Store, where my father was told, he was highly regarded.

When he was a young man, my father was the life and soul of the party; he loved playing cards and billiards and was very sociable. The neighbours would always call for him when they were going out for the night. By the late 1940s, he had joined the Irish Army and was stationed in Limerick but, after meeting my mother when he was home on leave, he decided not to return. Instead, he went back to work with the farmers around Tralee while they courted.

MY MOTHER, Margaret Teahan, was always known as Peggy. She was born in 1923 in Milltown in the centre of County Kerry and was one of a family of four children. She was the only girl; her brothers were Paddy, John and Donie. Her father, Dan, who was born in 1896, worked at the Presentation Convent in the village, looking after both the house and the garden. Her mother, Hannah Moriarty, worked in the home and was a great dressmaker. My grandmother bought a Singer sewing machine for £5 when my mother was a small child. She would make clothes for her own family and for the neighbours, although she didn't sew as a business. My mother said she was one of the best dressed girls going out. She often told me about a lemon-coloured dress that her mother made for her; everyone admired it and she was delighted to be wearing such a beautiful dress made by her beloved mother. Unlike my father, my mother's earliest days were happy and secure; my grandfather had a regular job and income and my grandmother was a great homemaker.

Tragedy, however, was lying in wait for the Teahan family and struck them viciously. When my mother was twelve, her father contracted tuberculosis (TB) and died on the 26th of May 1938. This disease, commonly known as consumption, was rampant in Ireland in the 1920s and 1930s. It was deadly and incurable, like AIDS in its earliest days. It was (and still is in certain parts of the world) a highly contagious disease which claimed the lives of both the weak and the strong. When TB first hit the Teahan family, the vaccination to counter it was not yet readily available in Ireland.

Within a short space of time, the disease struck the family again: Paddy, who worked in Larkin's Bakery in Milltown along with his brother John, contracted it. By then, a sanatorium for TB sufferers had opened in Edenburn Hospital near Castleisland town. The Bon Secours Sisters ran the sanatorium which provided the only treatment then available in the country which consisted of fresh air, total rest, two pints of Guinness daily and nutritious food. It wasn't until the 1950s that incidences of TB began to decline in Ireland following the heroic efforts of Dr Noel Browne, whose parents had died of TB and who had himself contracted the disease in 1940. It was another twenty years before it was almost fully eradicated in the country.

But that was too late for Paddy who died in 1944 when he was twenty-two. Their mother was next; she, too, went to Edenburn but didn't survive and died on the 31st of August 1945. Next was John who lost his young life to the disease in 1948, also at the age of twenty-two. By the time my mother was twenty-four, both her parents and two brothers had succumbed to TB. All that was left were herself and Donie, the youngest member of the family. Their profound grief at the loss of their parents and brothers was intensified by the hurt they felt following their ostracisation in their local area. Nobody would call to their home or come near them in case they, too, caught the killer disease. This wasn't unusual as people were afraid that they could contract TB even by talking to someone who had it, or whose family members had it.

My mother and Donie decided their only option was to leave Milltown and move away from the neighbourhood. In 1949, they packed up only three belongings—a knife, a sweeping brush and my grandmother's Singer sewing machine—and made their way to Tralee. Both of them worked on O'Loughlin's farm just outside the town. Donie stayed on there when my mother left after getting a job as a housekeeper with the McSweeneys, a Tralee business family.

Despite the tragedy that marked her life, my mother, who was an attractive, young woman, wanted to make a new family for herself. She and my father met at a dance in Tralee. She was very good at dancing and he was a fabulous dancer and this common interest united them.

They had both already experienced extreme harshness in their lives—she through illness and death and he through poverty—and I think this also gave them a shared bond. They got married and set up home in Tralee in a rented room in Kevin Barry's Villas, Ballymullen.

I WAS BORN in May 1950 and the following year my brother Danny was born. With the family expanding, my parents decided they needed more space and we moved to Manor, a few miles outside the town of Tralee. We lived there until 1956, by which time the family had continued to grow; Joseph was born in 1952, Joan in 1953 and Áine in 1955. The house in Manor was large and three families lived there. A family with two children occupied a room at the front of the house and my mother got on exceptionally well with Mrs Tangney, the woman who lived there. A mother and daughter lived in another room beside the Tangneys and we lived in a room at the back of the house.

Everything we owned was in the one room. There were two double beds with a table in the middle of the room. There was also a cot and a drawer for the baby. A cupboard near the room was used for storing food and clothes and we also kept turf and kindling there for the fire that would be lit in the open fireplace. A clothesline was placed around the fireplace where my mother would hang the washing to dry. There was no toilet and no running water and we had to go to a nearby well for our water supply. Just outside our room was a stairs that led to another bedroom but we were not allowed up there because my mother was terrified that we might fall down the stairs. Of course, we sneaked up to have a look; there was an iron bed in the room and, strangely, a lot of trench coats.

Even though she had a young family, my mother continued to work in McSweeney's a number of days each week. She'd bring a couple of us to work with her while my father would mind the others. Her employers were brilliant to her, especially 'Mrs Mac', as she was known locally; she would give her any extra food to take home. Their house had a beautiful long hallway and a dining room where my mother would light the fire before cooking dinner in the evening. She was a great housekeeper and cook; she'd bake bread for the family, which they loved. Mrs Mac had two brothers who were Jesuit priests and when they came home on holiday, they'd give my mother a couple of pounds.

Her birthday was on the 3rd of January and one year she got a lovely Christmas cake from Mrs Mac. It was covered in white icing and had a red feathered wrapper around it. I can still see that cake, sitting beside my grandmother's Singer sewing machine just inside the door of our room. 'When your mother comes home this evening, we'll light the cake,' my father said. We didn't have candles to put on it so we used lighted matches instead. When we heard her coming up the stairs we got ready and, as soon as she opened the door, we sang 'Happy Birthday'; she was delighted.

My parents seldom socialised together once the children started arriving but I do remember the time they went to

Puck Fair in Killorglin. They got a babysitter and headed off, dressed up—ironically—as tramps for a fancy dress competition that was taking place at the fair. They won and had a choice of prizes. My mother insisted on choosing a golliwog for me and so I became the delighted owner of a golliwog doll with a black face and red hands that was way bigger than me. But the happy times were rare as it became more and more apparent that my father was not going to be a proper provider for the family.

He was still working as a farm labourer but he wasn't too concerned about going to work every day and, even when he did go, he didn't bring his pay home for the family. It was up to my mother to ensure there was food to feed us and money to buy the basic necessities. His socialising, drinking and card playing began to impact negatively on the growing family in these years, making life more and more difficult. He also became increasingly aggressive and would turn on us children for no reason at all. My mother was a strict disciplinarian, but there was no reasoning with my father. He was a dab hand at hitting us with a stick that was kept over the fireplace and wouldn't stop until he'd really hurt you.

UNCLE DONIE, my mother's brother, worked nearby and visited us regularly, always bringing lollipops for the children. He and my mother were very close, bonded together not only by family ties but also by the tragedy they'd suffered when they lost all their family to TB. When he stayed over, Donie slept in the room at the top of the stairs. In 1954, he became ill and stayed with us more often so that my mother could keep a watch over him. He became sicker and sicker and was soon staying upstairs all the time. The full horror of what was happening soon dawned on both Donie and my mother: he had contracted TB. They were both devastated but he refused to go to Edenburn sanatorium, saying that he didn't want to die there.

This was a terrible time in our lives; my father, who got on very well with Donie, was afraid we would all catch TB and the situation became very tense. I've no doubt my mother harboured the same fears but she couldn't turn her back on her last remaining sibling who was weakening by the day and petrified of dying alone in the sanatorium. No matter what she said, he refused to go in there. My last memory of Donie is of him sitting on a stone outside the house with a pillow under him, waiting to be taken away. I didn't know where he was going but I do know that he died soon after, on May Day 1955, at the age of twenty-six. We had no money for his funeral but the O'Loughlins— his employers—paid for his burial. The tragedy is that had Donie gone to Edenburn, he would probably have survived because, by that stage, treatment for the disease had improved significantly.

My mother was devastated after her last remaining sibling died; she didn't talk about him in our presence but would go to Mrs Tangney's room where we could hear her crying and talking about her brother who had been such a lovely man. 'Nothing worse can happen to me now,' I heard her say. The extreme loss she experienced caused her to create a shell around her to try and protect herself. From that time, she seldom cuddled us or showed us affection and could be tough and hard though I never doubted she had our best interests at heart.

I STARTED SCHOOL in Moyderwell in September 1955, walking the twenty-five minute journey there morning and evening. My mother used to check my bag each night to make sure that what she had bought—pencil, pencil pointer and copy—was still in the bag. She had so little money that she couldn't afford to replace anything. One night when she checked my bag she saw a different pencil pointer in it. She got angry and told me that I was never, ever to take anything that belonged to someone else. 'Nobody steals,' she said. 'That is the one thing you do not do.' It was a lesson that stayed with me throughout my life, even when I didn't abide by it. It was many years later when the truth of her words really came back to haunt me.

Within a few weeks of starting school, I got sick. TB had struck the family again in the same year that Donie died. I was taken away in an ambulance, accompanied by a nurse who promised me that I would get a doll at the place we were going to. I was only five and a half and had no idea what was happening. After what seemed like hours, I sat up and looked out the window and saw ships. Soon after, we arrived in the coastal town of Foynes in County Limerick and I was taken to the hospital there. The first thing I did when I was brought inside was ask for the doll I'd been promised but there was no doll.

The hospital had originally been built as a luxury hotel for the flying boat passengers that visited Foynes. When the flying boats stopped coming in, the hotel became a hospital. I was there for about ten months during which time my brother Danny beacame a patient there as well. By then, the treatment for TB had advanced to the point that there was a good chance of survival once you got fresh air, good food and rest. We were given lessons and shown films and had other activities. I remember getting chickenpox and having cardboard put on my hands and arms to prevent me from scratching my face. I never recalled anything negative about my time there other than the fact that I was away from my family and didn't have any visitors.

In August 1956, I returned home and met Áine, the latest addition to the family, who had been born shortly after I'd gone to Foynes the previous year. I went back to school and every week Nurse Lenihan, the district nurse, would call to check on the family. This was common practice in families where TB had struck. She said that my mother was the best woman she'd ever met for cleanliness and looking after her children, but she knew that she had no support. My mother got vouchers to buy food that would help build up our strength. She would bring these into the shop to exchange for porridge, butter and milk and while she always got food, she would buy cigarettes as well. Throughout their lives, both my parents smoked heavily despite trying to give them up at various times. For my mother, they seemed, at times, to be her only source of solace.

THE FAMILY was growing yet my father wasn't helping out and my mother was coming under increasing pressure. They often fought and when that happened I'd retreat into my own world where, in my mind, I created someone that I could talk with and who would make everything okay. I would tell my imaginary friend everything that was happening, and while I was in that world I was happy. The real world was more difficult and, as a young child, I often wondered why my parents couldn't stop arguing and just be happy. One night there was a particularly big fight. I heard my mother saying that she had no money and couldn't manage anymore; that she couldn't put food on the table. 'Do what you like,' was my father's response. I could tell from her voice that she was at breaking point. Eventually I fell asleep and when I woke up the following morning, my mother, who was pregnant again, was gone and had taken the baby with her.

I asked my father where she was and he said she had gone to stay with Nana Grady, her aunt who lived in Tralee. It was the first time I remember my mother leaving the family home and I could see he was in a bit of a state. He asked Mrs Tangney to keep an eye on us while he went to his mother's. When he returned he told us to pack our meagre belongings. He got the loan of a van and soon we were leaving Manor and heading towards Nan's house, our new home. My siblings and I travelled in the van with my father in total confusion about what was happening in our young lives.

NAN'S HOUSE was in Caherleaheen, right beside the local national school. The house was a two-bedroom cottage with an iron roof. There were two red pillars at the gate and three steps led down to the front door which opened into the kitchen which was the main room in the house. There was one bedroom to the right and one to the left of the main room, with a scullery at the back. Nan had moved to this house after marrying Paddy Sugrue and she'd always had some one of her adult children living there with her. When we arrived, my father's stepsister Bridie was living there with her children. Her husband had died following an accident while working on the railway and she'd stayed on with Nan even though she'd received compensation and had bought a two-storey house in Tralee town.

The first night we arrived, we had to sleep in Nan's bedroom because there were so many in the house. Bridie left soon afterwards and my father and the four of us that were with him moved into the newly vacated bedroom. There was a lot of talk between my father and Nan and after about three days my mother appeared with Áine. I was delighted that she was back and hoped that there wouldn't be any more fighting.

The room we lived in was tiny. The walls were very damp and the floorboards were rotten; in fact, before we'd moved in, the house had been condemned but we had nowhere else to go. I couldn't understand why we'd left the room in Manor—which was much bigger and had a fireplace as well—but we were here now and had to make the best of it. Seven of us shared the room initially, soon to become eight when the next baby was born.

Normally we ate in the room we slept in, not in the kitchen. We only ate there if Nan invited us, or if my mother was at work and Nan knew we wouldn't be fed. There was a little hole in the bedroom door and you could look through that and see into the kitchen. I'd do the peeping and would be able to gauge what kind of form Nan was in. She suffered from lumbago and this made her grumpy at times. If she was in bad form, she'd be sitting by the fire, talking to herself. If she was in good form, my mother might go up to the kitchen and they would have a cup of tea together.

My father was a bit better behaved now that he was under his mother's roof. He cut timber and went to the bog but he remained mostly irresponsible. Nan would reprimand him on occasion when he'd come home drunk, saying, 'Paddy, why didn't you come home last night? Don't you know the children are depending on you? Why did you go playing cards?'. While things improved between himself and my mother, mainly, I think, because he was aware there were other adults in the house and he didn't want them to overhear any fighting, he still wouldn't go to work regularly. He might work the odd day but the problem was he wouldn't bring his wages home. There was a local hall nearby where billiards were played and coming up to Christmas players could win prizes. My father won a hamper one year and there was jubilation in the house when that happened. He went out most nights, to local rambling houses if he didn't have any money and into town if he had a bit of cash to drink, play cards and billiards.

My mother started work at nine and finished at seven. A next-door neighbour would give her a drive to work and the Macs would drive her home in the evening. When she was at home, she was always busy scrubbing, cleaning and washing. At night, she would join Nan at the fireplace if Nan's form was good. My mother didn't have any friends although she got on extremely well with the McSweeneys, who were very fond of her.

I think she was a broken woman before ever she got married and then, when Donie died, that really pushed her over the edge into a place of sadness. That, coupled with the poverty that we couldn't get out of, made her life very tough. She was earning about £1 a day and had eight mouths to feed. It was pure grinding poverty.

FROM THE TIME we moved into Nan's house, the first thing I did every morning was go to a local farmer to buy a gallon of milk. The farmer's wife would always offer me bread with blackcurrant jam, a treat I never refused. I then had to go to the well for water, a task I did mostly on my own even though I was terrified as I had to cross a river using stepping stones and was afraid that I would fall in and drown. Sometimes I had to go to the well three times a day. The odd time, my brother Danny, who was a year younger than me, would come with me. I remember using the handle of the brush so we could carry two buckets and, hopefully, not have to make another trip that day. There was a barrel outside in the yard that collected rainwater which was used to wash the clothes. Some mornings I had to go to the shop for cigarettes and oil, or maybe a half pound of butter. Then I helped my mother get the others up and ready for the day before we headed off to school.

For breakfast we would have porridge and we used to take a bit of bread and jam to school where we got cocoa to drink. I helped prepare mugs of the hot drink for the children to have with a bit of bread with jam or sugar on top. There was no such thing as butter for us; it was a non-existent luxury. We'd have potatoes when we came home. I remember having cow's heart on a Sunday; my Nan would stuff it and that was supposed to be a big treat even though I didn't like it. Sometimes we'd have a bit of bacon and I'd go to a neighbour's field to get a head of cabbage or a turnip. I often went down and dug up a few potatoes as well when we were stuck.

Although my mother didn't go to Mass every Sunday, she had great faith and prayed a lot to St Anthony and St Martin. She said that you didn't have to beat down the door to the church every Sunday and that a prayer was just as good. The rosary was a must for her every night. My father never went to Mass and Nan would go only occasionally but the whole family would go at Christmas. Although we were poor, we always had something special at that time of the year such as jam, barm-brack or currant cake. We would have goose which Nan would cook and we'd all have Christmas dinner together in the kitchen; the children would be fed first and then the adults would sit down and eat.

We would always get something from Santa, no matter how small it was. The girls might get a tiny doll in a bath. I remember one of the boys getting a cowboy suit and another getting a ball. You'd get one present and that was it. I remember one Christmas, when I was eight years old and my mother had no money whatsoever. A woman gave her some toys that had belonged to her children. There was no present for me and my mother decided she had to tell me about Santa. She asked me to help her with the wrapping and broke the news as gently as she could. Although I was deeply disappointed I was excited that there would be something for all the other children; my happiness depended very much on theirs.

MY MOTHER never had to worry about the house from when I was six years old because I did everything. I changed the children, I washed the floor and I'd be delighted in the evening when she'd come home and I'd say, 'Mom, look what I did for you'. It was like I was a substitute mother because I was the eldest. The other children weren't helping out at this stage; the next in age to me, Danny and Joseph, were always playing so the responsibility fell to me. If the children wanted anything they put their hands up for me, not my mother or father. Consequently, if anything happened to them, I'd be blamed.

I felt the pressure of my responsibilities, often to my own detriment. There was one morning when I was returning home having bought the milk for breakfast from a local farmer. I fell and all the milk spilled in a pool around me;

its whiteness turned pink as the blood from my badly cut knee mixed with it. A neighbour had heard me scream when I fell and she came to my aid. She was concerned about my knee but my main concern was that I'd spilled all the milk and was facing home with none for the breakfast. She gave me what milk she had because it was a long walk back to the farmer's and I was after paying six pence for the milk that was now on the ground and there was no extra money to buy more. I was afraid to tell my mother about my fall so I just carried on as if nothing had happened though I was in bad pain.

The only place I could relax was at school, although my desire to please was apparent there also and I worked hard to do well. The school was very close to Nan's house, only a few minutes' walk away. It was a two-teacher school, with one room for the juniors and the other for the seniors. Master Caball was the headmaster and he taught the seniors while Miss O'Loughlin taught the juniors. There were about forty pupils in the entire school at the time, with five in my class and I got on great with them.

I was an average student; neither the best nor the worst in the class. Learning was easy enough for me once I applied myself, and I was interested in applying myself because I really wanted to do well. Books were handed down from one class to the next and it was seldom that you'd have to buy a new book. I loved Irish, maths and history though I didn't like English or geography. I do remember, however, winning a competition one time for an essay with the title, 'What would you do if you won £5?'. I wrote that if I won the money, I'd buy a second-hand bike so that I could get around faster and do errands quicker.

There was a playground for the smaller pupils and another one for the older girls and boys. I was spending so much of my time with small children that I wanted to play tag, 'hit' and statues with the bigger ones just to have a bit of fun. Even though many of the pupils hated school, it was where I got to play with other children so I didn't mind going there at all.

In the evening after school we had to change from our 'good' clothes into our rags and do our homework. We didn't have a uniform but we put on the rags when we came home to keep our school clothes clean. If my mother was out working, the baby would have her two arms up for me to take her out of the pram. I would change and wash her and put clothes on her. I knew there was no point in going outside with my friends; I wouldn't be out five minutes before I'd be called back inside.

I was friends with the girls who lived next door to us. One was ahead of me at school while the other was in my class and I went to their house whenever I could. Their father worked in town while their mother was a housewife. I enjoyed going into their home where there was harmony and stability. The main attraction, though, was the food; when I'd pass their house in the evening, I could see the table set for tea. In fairness to the girls' mother, she regularly invited me in for supper and I was given whatever the girls were having. I also got their clothes when they had outgrown them. I didn't question why things were like this except when it came to the food; I would why we didn't have the kind of food they had.

While I loved being at school, I clearly remember an incident that happened when I was in the junior class that upset me very much. A bike that belonged to a pupil went missing and a woman whose children attended the school told me she'd give me money if I said that a particular boy had taken the bike. I hadn't witnessed the theft but was so tempted by the thought of the money I told my teacher what I'd been asked to say. Within a short time, she started ignoring me in the classroom and this upset me greatly.

I was a diligent pupil and to be ostracised in this way hurt me greatly. I felt there wasn't anybody at home that I could turn to. My mother was in hospital at the time and I was afraid to tell my father or Nan; they would have been really upset with me for telling a lie. Also, I'd taken money off this woman to tell a lie—even though I hadn't known at the time that it was a lie—so I felt I had done wrong.

After about a week, I went to a neighbour. She was a teenage girl and I told her what was happening. Although she had left the primary school years earlier, she went there and spoke to my teacher, explaining to her what I couldn't explain myself. Then the teacher brought me to one side and had a chat with me. She asked me why I'd done it. 'Because I was asked to,' I replied, explaining that the woman had given me money. The teacher left the issue lie then because the woman in question was good to the school and gave support in times when schools didn't have much money. For my own part, I learned the valuable lesson that you should never put a price on honesty.

One of my happiest school memories is of the day of my First Holy Communion. My mother got my rigout from Mrs Mac and I felt like a princess when I was dressed up. The only thing she had to buy for me was new shoes and I was thrilled to get a shiny black patent pair. Our substitute class teacher, a Miss Curtin from Dingle, invited the communicants and their parents to her house for a meal after the ceremony. There was a tablecloth on the table and everything was ready; I was intrigued at how she'd managed to have the meal ready as she had been at the Holy Communion ceremony in the church, but it was her mother that had cooked it.

We were served a fabulous Irish breakfast, including sausages, rashers, an egg and a tomato. I couldn't believe that someone would put food on a plate for you and all you had to do was sit down and eat it. I was watching what everyone else was doing for fear I'd make a mistake with the knives and forks; it was as good as being in a restaurant.

That was a beautiful day. It was also the first time I had been taken anywhere on an outing. Another first was the fact that my mother and I got to spend the day together with no other child present. I think that was the real highlight for me; I had all her attention and she made a big fuss of me. We stayed out until about six o'clock and walked home from town that evening. I made nineteen shillings and six pence that day. A woman gave me half a crown and said to make sure I said a prayer for her, which I did.

The following Sunday when I was going to Mass with my mother, we found a six-penny bit and a gold three-penny bit at the bottom of the Communion bag. I was amazed because we had turned that bag upside down the previous week to make sure we had all the money. Nine pence was a lot to us. My mother took most of my collection but I didn't have a problem with that. I was allowed to keep a small amount and I bought myself a timber pencil case with it.

When I progressed to the senior classes, I started to come in early to school to do some jobs. My first job each day was to light the fire in the classroom. That time there were no firelighters but we had an oblong-shaped block with a wire handle that you'd soak in paraffin oil in a two-pound jam jar. I had to ensure this was done each evening so I could light the fire the following morning after I'd cleaned out the ashes. I'd pray to God that the fire would light because if the turf was damp it mightn't. After that, I'd sweep the room. There was a third room in the school building where we had lunch and where I made the cocoa.

BY 1959, we had been three years at Nan's and were settled into life there. I was well used to looking after all my siblings, helping out and generally acting like a young adult in the house even though I was only nine years old. But I was happy to help my mother and I enjoyed spending time with Nan and also with my Uncle Johnny who was a lovely man. He lived in the house with us, leaving early each morning to go to work and returning in the evening to eat before heading out to one of the local rambling houses. While he liked a drink and to play cards, he was not a bit like my father.

Sometime in the early summer of that year, my mother became ill. At first she just seemed more tired than usual but, one day, my father came into the kitchen where I was with Nan and started crying. 'Peggy is going to Edenburn,' he said. TB had struck the family again. My mother, the last surviving member of the Teahan family, had finally succumbed to the disease that had killed all her immediate family. Even though I'd had TB when I was six, I didn't understand what my father was saying. The only word that made any sense was 'burn' and I ran out to where one of my brothers was playing, shouting hysterically, 'They're going to burn Mom!'.

Things happened very fast after that. We didn't see my mother before she went to the sanatorium. Within a day of her leaving, some people arrived at Nan's in a big vehicle. It was the 'cruelty man' and a nurse who had come to take all the children away and put them in care. It was raining heavily and my Nan and father and all of the children, including myself, were in the kitchen. The adults spoke to each other. My father was asked our names and ages and, while he got the names right, he didn't know our correct ages. I asked what was happening. 'Ye are all going somewhere else to live,' he said. 'Your Mom is gone to hospital for a long time,' Nan explained. 'I can't mind you all so you have to go until she comes back.'

I couldn't believe what was happening. 'I'm not going,' I shouted and ran out the back door. I kept running until

I had crossed at least two fields and, finally, I hid in the middle of a bunch of high nettles and stayed there. I heard my father roaring my name but I didn't move. I just sat in the rain and waited. I don't know how long I was in hiding but, eventually, I came out. I was like a drowned rat; it was wet and cold and I was miserable. I sneaked back into the house quietly and met Nan. I asked her where my father was. She said he had to go and sign the court order for the others. I looked at her in fear. 'You're alright,' she said, 'you can stay with me. It was then I noticed that Joan, who was six, was also in the house. For some reason, she hadn't been taken away.

Two brothers and two sisters were taken to Killarney where a court order was processed and where my father signed them into the care of institutions run by religious orders. The boys were sent to St Joseph's Industrial School in Tralee while the girls went to the Mercy-run Nazareth House, which was across the road from St Joseph's. In 1959, the oldest boy was eight and the younger boy was seven and they both stayed in St Joseph's until they were sixteen. One of the girls was three when she went into care and the other one was just under two. They remained in the Nazareth until 1970. The entire family never lived together again.

It was my mother who'd phoned the 'cruelty man', as he was called, once she realised that she had TB and needed long-term care. She wanted to make sure that her children would have a clean bed and that they would be fed, and she guessed that wasn't going to happen under my father's care. She knew in her heart and soul that he couldn't look after us and that he was an unfit father. It was an extreme action to take but her life was so hard and she had no real support; she had no sister, no brother, no mother, no father. She was in a situation where she had no control over her personal life, forced to have children that she couldn't afford, and barely keeping her head above water financially. To send her children into care was a devastating decision for my mother to have to make but she made it in the belief that it was in our best interests.

She probably thought that she wouldn't survive the TB even though treatment had improved, but, as all her family had already died, it would have been difficult for her to be optimistic. Even if she didn't die, she knew that treatment was long, usually about two years in a sanatorium. By 1959, Nan's house was already condemned by the authorities and the damp walls and cramped living conditions undoubtedly exacerbated my mother's condition.

Nurse Lenihan would have been a regular visitor to us from the time that my brother and I had contracted TB three years earlier. She liked my mother and would make sure to call to see if she was okay because she knew what she was putting up with. My mother loved to see her coming even though she was worried about what Nan would say. A lot of people hated to have the district nurse calling to their homes because she was so strict, especially if the place was dirty. She'd say that a person might be poor but there was no need for dirt. While we were very poor and had very little, the house was always spotless and the beds were always clean. I'm sure that once my mother was diagnosed with TB she discussed what to do with Nurse Lenihan. In fact, she was the nurse that came to the house with the 'cruelty man' the day my brothers and sisters were taken into care.

THE HOUSE felt very empty with my mother and most of my siblings gone. Now there was just me, Joan, Nan, my father and Uncle Johnny. I was so used to looking after the small ones that I didn't really know what to do with myself when I got home from school. I was glad that I didn't have to go to the well so often, but it was very lonely. However, Nan was good to me and made sure that I had enough to eat and that I did my lessons. But then, about a month after my mother went to Edenburn, Nan got sick and told me that Joan and I would be moving to Tralee to live at my step-aunt's. There was never any question of my father looking after his own children.

Once I got used to the idea, I was delighted to be moving in with my step-aunt and three cousins. They lived in a two-storey house in the town. When you entered, there was a hallway with a door to the left-hand side which led to the sitting room. There was a kitchen which had a range and beside it was a big scullery where you could cook and eat. Out the back there was a tiny garden with a shed. Upstairs, there were three rooms and a toilet. My step-aunt shared a bedroom with her daughter, her sons were in another bedroom and Joan and I shared the third bedroom. It was the first time I'd lived in a house that had indoor plumbing and electricity. They had a television and I loved watching *Tolka Row*; this was a totally new experience for me.

I was quite happy at first and busied myself cleaning and tidying. I had always been busy at Nan's; it became a kind of coping strategy for me so I did the same in my step-aunt's. Also, I wanted to be good and to please people. But no matter what I did, I could see that they preferred Joan, who was a particularly beautiful child. Gypsy women would call to the house and the family would always buy a dress for Joan but never buy one for me. She was allowed stay up late while I had to go to bed around eight o'clock, even though she was younger than me. I couldn't understand this and resented it. It's not that I never got anything but I had a really strong sense of not being special in any way.

But Joan wasn't with me for long. Within a short space of time, she got sick. It was TB again, and she was taken to the hospital in Foynes where I'd been with my brother three years earlier. Another one of my sisters, who was in the Nazareth, also contracted the illness at that time so they ended up in Foynes together. After their treatment in the hospital both of them were returned to the Nazareth where they spent the rest of their youth.

FOR THE FIRST TIME in my life, I was living in a house without any of my siblings. I was still trying to be responsible and keep some semblance of normality in my life but I was living in a house where things were quite

different to what I'd been used to. At weekends, my step-
aunt and some of my cousins would be up all night and
in bed much of the day. They would gather in the sitting
room with visitors and drink bottles of stout and chat
until the late hours. My step-aunt's five older children
were all in England and they sent some money home to
their mother. I don't ever remember being hungry while
I lived there but I nearly always had to prepare the food
myself. I was regularly sent to the shop, not only for the
family but also for the neighbours. 'You don't have to write
it down. Breeda will remember the list in her head,' they'd
say. I'd feel good when they said something nice about me.

I was still trying to do the right thing and be a normal
ten-year-old, but it was tough. I went to school in the town
but I didn't make any friends there. I was a country girl,
away from all my immediate family, and I trusted nobody;
I kept everything to myself. They thought I was brilliant at
school even though I was only average. The classes were
so big and as the numbers had been so small in my old
school, I had learned much more and was ahead of the
other pupils. They didn't like me for that. Between my
lack of friends and the fact that nobody seemed to care
whether or not I turned up, I missed a lot of schooling
during my time in Tralee.

On Sunday nights, my father would come into town
to play cards and I'd watch for him out of my bedroom
window. When I saw him passing, I'd want to throw myself
out the window, trying to get to him to ask him to please
take me back to Nan's. But I couldn't open the window

and he never called to visit. He didn't visit the others in St Joseph's or the Nazareth either.

I HAD no contact with my mother; none of her children were allowed visit her during her time at Edenburn. However, letters did come to my step-aunt's house from her and I loved to see an envelope with her handwriting on it. By Christmas 1960, she was sufficiently recovered that she was going to be allowed out for a visit. It wasn't a good idea for her to go to Nan's as the house was so damp, especially the room we had lived in, so my mother wrote to my step-aunt asking if she could stay at her house during her few days away from the sanatorium.

I heard my step-aunt talking about the letter from my perch at the top of the stairs. Her tone was one of 'Who does she think she is? I'm going to write her a letter and put her in her place. There is a fear of her; she is well fed, warm and being taken care of and now she wants me to put her up over the Christmas'. I was on the watch-out for the letter that my step-aunt wrote to my mother and one day when I was cleaning the kitchen I found it behind the radio. It was in an envelope with my mother's name was on it. I destroyed the letter because I didn't want my mother to get it.

When my step-aunt asked me if I had seen it, I said I hadn't. But she wrote another one and made sure to post it. The only upside was that now I knew my mother would be coming to Nan's for Christmas and I was determined to meet her there. I found out what day she was arriving and said to my step-aunt that I was going out to see my mother and that I'd be back that evening. The truth was that I was determined to never return.

I WALKED the three miles to Nan's house with joy in my step. When I got there my mother had already arrived. I was over the moon to see her again and she hugged me closely. She looked so well; she was wearing a lovely brown skirt and had put on a bit of weight which gave her a bloom I'd rarely seen. Nan was in great form, too, as was my father. I found out Mom would be staying for a few days and I begged her to let me stay with her for that time. Mom and Nan agreed and I was able to relax for a bit and enjoy being with my mother for the first time in a year and a half.

One of the first things she did was cut my hair which was covered in nits; she could see immediately that I wasn't being properly looked after in Tralee. I didn't tell her everything about my life there, but she guessed enough to know that I shouldn't go back. I told her that I didn't want to return. There was some talk about me going to the Nazareth House where my sisters were. I had no intention of going in there either: I'd seen enough of the inside of that place when I visited the girls to know that I didn't want to go there so I pleaded with Nan to let me stay with her. I told her that I was old enough to look after myself and that I really wanted to come back to school in Caherleaheen because I wasn't learning anything in Tralee.

It was finally agreed that I could stay on when my mother went back to Edenburn. I settled back in very quickly at Nan's. I was the only child there with Nan, my father and Uncle Johnny and I shared a room with my grandmother, sleeping at the bottom of her bed. I was much happier there and was soon back getting water from the well, going to the shop and doing all the jobs I'd done previously, but the workload was much lighter than before because all the younger ones were gone.

CHAPTER TWO

DISCOVERING THE WIDER WORLD

WHEN MY MOTHER went back to Edenburn in early January 1961, we thought she'd be spending at least another year there. However, because she had become pregnant during her visit home at Christmas, she left the sanatorium before she began to show and returned to Nan's in June of that year. In total, she spent around two years in Edenburn. My father had visited her the odd time and some cousins came from England to visit her too. She also had a cousin from Killarney who would call to see her every so often.

In that two-year period, she didn't see any of her children except me when we met at Nan's during her Christmas visit home in 1960. A Sister and a Brother from the two care homes where my siblings were would write to tell her how the children were getting on and she'd write back to them. The only time I was in Edenburn was the day my mother was coming home when a neighbour drove my father and myself there to collect her.

It was great to have Mom home again and four months after she returned, my second youngest sister was born.

My mother returned to work in McSweeney's and she'd take the baby with her when she went in there. It was always my greatest desire that the family would all be together again someday but whenever I asked if the others were coming home she would say, 'Not yet, we can't do that yet'.

I WAS happy to be back at Caherleaheen national school although I was one of the only pupils that liked it in those days because of the master. He had a temper and was quick to use the rod. From a young age, however, I could read adults very well and I was always able to read the master's moods, even from the way he got out of his car. If his face was white he was in a bad mood; if he had a colour in it he was in a good mood. If his form was positive, I'd say 'Good morning' and offer to make a cup of tea for him, otherwise I'd keep my distance.

During all my time at school, I only got slapped once. When that happened, I was very upset and went home crying. Later, when he met my mother, the master said, 'I gave Breeda a slap and I will never forget her face as long as I live; she was absolutely shocked'. He said that he didn't want to do it but felt that he had to punish me; such were the education methods back then. On Fridays, when I was in the senior classes, my mother and I would clean the school, work that she didn't get paid for. However, everybody was contributing in some way, mostly by donating turf or wood to heat the building. Our contribution was to clean the classrooms of a Friday because we couldn't afford to bring anything in.

In 1962, I made my confirmation and took the name Maria Goretti. A neighbour made a lovely blue and white dress for me. It had a white collar, white cuffs and a white pleated band around the middle that tied at the back with fasteners. The neighbour also made a coat for me out of an old navy tweed coat that she had. I remember it clearly with its navy velvet collar, buttons down the front and a little flare at the end. I also did my primary certificate in the June of that year. I passed well in English, Irish and maths. One day when I was doing one of the exams, I had to bring the baby into school with me. She was about one at the time and there was nobody at home to mind her. The junior class teacher took her while I did the exam. I was back in my old role, taking responsibility for the babies again.

The young children at school always called me 'Momma Breeda' because I looked after them the same way I looked after my siblings. When my own brothers and sisters were taken from the house I was traumatised and missed them so much that the teachers would encourage the younger pupils to go to me whenever they wanted to be minded or comforted. Before I left national school, I was presented with a book as an award for being the most caring person in the school.

I spent the summer months after leaving national school living and working in Killarney. My mother's cousin Timmy lived in Muckross with his wife and family where they had a farm. He had worked in the Fáilte Hotel in Killarney town and said he could get me a job there for the summer. My mother was thrilled because it meant that I'd be earning a bit of money. I started by working in the kitchen cleaning the pots and pans but I didn't like that. One day I made an apple tart to let them see what I could do and then they allowed me help out with the food preparation and making desserts. This was good of the chef seen as I'd forgotten to put the sugar in that tart and had to sprinkle lots of it on top instead! I'd stay overnight in the hotel if I had to work late; they had rooms for their employees and I loved staying over. I even sneaked out one or two nights with the other girls to go to a dance. On my days off, I'd help Timmy and his family bringing in the hay. It was a wonderful summer.

THE CLOSEST secondary school to us was in Moyderwell in Tralee and it was there I went in September 1962. I had already spent some time at this school when I'd lived at my step-aunt's. I'd hated my time in the primary school part of the building and didn't like the time I spent in the secondary school much more. I still didn't have a bicycle and would walk the three miles there and back if I didn't get a lift from one of the neighbours who'd be driving to town for work. I found the transition to secondary school difficult as I was the only one of my classmates to go to Moyderwell and knew nobody there. It was also strange to go into a much bigger class compared to the primary school where there had been just five of us in the one year. All the teachers were nuns and some of them were very nice but I didn't make any friends among the pupils.

I was much happier when I was working at McSweeney's Auctioneer & Valuers, Grocery & Publican in Lower Castle Street, Tralee. I'd started working there part-time during my final year at national school. I'd go to their premises in the evenings during the week and also on Saturdays, when Brigid, the full-time shop assistant, wasn't there. When I was coming to the end of my first year at secondary school, Brigid handed in her notice when she got married and moved to another town. When her full-time position came up, I took it without a second thought, so ending my formal education at the age of fourteen. There was a new addition to our family that year as well when my youngest sister was born.

THE McSWEENEYS were a successful business family who, at one time, had owned the Ashe Memorial Hall and the Picturedrome. When I started work full time with them in 1964, they had a shop, bar, auctioneers and travel agency. Barney and Mrs Mac and their daughter worked in the business, and Mrs Mac also looked after their beautiful home with the help of my mother. At their premises in Castle Street, the shop was to the front at the right-hand side and you had to go through a pair of swinging doors to enter the bar. The travel agency was a tiny space across from the grocery and there was a phone there; the number was 95.

I found the whole idea of the travel agency very exotic and was enthralled when people came in to book their tickets to England, Spain or America. There was also good business from those who went annually on pilgrimage to Lourdes in France. Barney did the auctioneering, either in the bar or in the travel agency area, noting everything down in a big book. Out the back was an area where they kept big sacks of Layers' Mash, chicken feed and potatoes. The business operated from Monday to Saturday, nine to six, with a half day on Wednesdays.

The shop was a very good general store which stocked everything the customer would need. In addition to the staples of bread, butter, milk and jam, I remember selling sultanas, Atora suet, Epsom salts, Milk of Magnesia, Andrew's Liver Salts, Gold Flake cigarettes, shoe polish, and laces. Tea was delivered in tea chests and I'd divide it into the quarter-pound, half-pound and pound bags. The sugar was also delivered loose and I'd bag that as well. In those days, they had bread that you would break into what were called 'hands' and people would ask for one or two hands of bread. Biscuits came in tins and people would ask for a bag of Nice, Kimberley, Mikado or Coconut Creams. The biscuits would be put in a brown paper bag and then you would weigh them. I'd often take one and let it melt in my mouth—my favourite were the Coconut Creams. I'd gone from having very little food in my life to being surrounded by it.

I dressed the window every second Monday. A sample of everything that was available for sale had to be put on display. Colours would fade in the sunshine so the items had to be replaced regularly. I also had to clean the two front windows, wash the floor and clean the bar.

Tralee was a busy market town in the 1960s and every Monday there was a mart and the farmers would come into McSweeney's afterwards. The customers, who were mainly country people, were lovely. I enjoyed working in the bar and talking to them. It was a nice place to work with a warm atmosphere.

I got seventeen and six a week when I started working full time. There were twenty shillings in a pound then and a pint of Guinness was one shilling and five pence. The pay wasn't great and Mrs Mac would give me two extra shillings when she was there. I'd go down to the Snackery restaurant and, for one and six, I'd get chips, beans and sausages. She told me to take lunch money when she wasn't present but I didn't feel comfortable doing that. I was afraid that Barney didn't know she had given me this permission and that he'd wonder what I was doing. Despite my reluctance, there were times when I was so hungry that I did take lunch money when Mrs Mac wasn't around.

I got paid on Friday and I'd always bring groceries home. I'd never had the opportunity to buy new clothes for myself before so when I had enough saved, I went into Sloane's drapery on Ashe Street. They allowed you pay for your purchases in weekly instalments and the first things I ever bought for myself were a grey skirt and a pink jumper. Every Friday, I'd go up to Sloane's and pay my weekly dues before walking home. I walked to work and home every day unless I was lucky enough to get a lift; I was as fit as a fiddle back then.

I was very fond of the McSweeneys and they had great affection for me. I loved all aspects of my job but the part I really adored was the auctioneering. Though there was an odd auction on Saturdays, Barney normally held his auctions on a Wednesday when the shop was shut for the half day. He'd drive to the venue and I'd beg him to take me along. The two of us would hit off in his car on Wednesday afternoons and, when the auction started, I'd position myself beside my boss to observe the bidders. I thought we must have looked an unlikely pairing, I was so small and he seemed so tall to me.

I was very good at noticing people signalling their bids and letting Barney know who had made the latest bid. He'd do the hammer and I always wanted to bang that hammer. With my little notebook, I felt a sense of purpose at these auctions; I felt that I was somehow helping out in a real and vital way. The fact is, Barney didn't have to bring anybody with him, but he saw my enthusiasm for the job and my presence did make it a bit easier for him. Wednesday was my half day, but I happily went with him and there was also the bonus that he might give me something if sales were good.

I didn't know at the time why I was so enthralled by the auctions; all I knew was that I really loved being in the thick of these events. It was only when I was a bit older that I understood that the buzz was the energy of the event itself, of watching people trying to outbid each other, stalling, bidding again and of observing the changing emotions on their faces. I could nearly tell what they were going to do before they knew themselves. There could be four or five bidding and then it would slow down, with people dropping out until there would be just two left, trying to outbid each other. Years later, when I started my own business, I realised that the seeds of my business acumen were sown on the farms and in the auction rooms of north Kerry where I travelled with Barney Mac.

At fifteen I was beginning to think about starting my own business. I wanted to better my prospects so I did a two-year supervisory and managerial course at the technical school in Tralee. The classes took place at night, from seven to nine, and I never missed one. However, when the time came to do the exams, I was struck down with the worst flu I'd ever had in my life. I don't know what came closer to killing me—the flu, or the fact that I never got to sit those exams which were so important to me.

I GOT to know people my own age in Tralee who were working in the shops in the town. There were girls working in the chemist's next door who were a year older than me. I loved hearing them talking about where they had been the night before. As I listened, I'd wish that I, too, had a social life and maybe a boyfriend. But I was still under the control of my parents who expected me to be home at a certain time and to hand over most of my wages. If I dawdled in town after work, I'd have to explain what I had been doing and who I had been talking to. My father was still not bringing in any money and, although my mother worked, she was earning very little. Adding more financial burden was the fact that, in 1965, she was pregnant again.

I was still very involved in minding my two youngest sisters who were at home. I would visit the others in the Nazareth and at St Joseph's on Sundays. I'd call to the boys first and then the girls. My mother rarely visited them and my father never called to see his children. I didn't ask them the reasons why at that time and, later on, I didn't feel comfortable broaching the subject with them. When they were a bit older, the boys were allowed out for the day and I loved to spend time with them at Nan's. All the time my siblings were in care, my greatest wish was that they would be brought home and we would all be together again under the one roof. I'd bring up the subject with my mother when I could, saying that now that I was working full time we'd be able to manage.

Nan's house was in a terrible state by then, with the walls seeping and floors rotting from the damp. My mother said there was no way we could bring the children back to those conditions. However, around the mid 1960s, the county council started to build some cottages not too far from where we were living. Now that there was another baby on the way, my mother applied for a council house. I was delighted. Nan's house had long been condemned and now, finally, we would have a new home and—I believed—we would all be together again.

In total, there were six houses built, close to Ballyseedy Woods on the old road into Tralee. Our family was made a priority, probably because of our history of TB and the fact that my mother was pregnant. That two young children were living in a condemned house most likely also influenced the council when it came to deciding who to put at the top of the list. Eventually, the first house was completed and we went to see it. I thought it was fabulous; there was electricity and running water and an outside toilet. The access road wasn't done but the house was ready for us to move into. However, there was no budging my parents. I asked and asked but they just wouldn't move. My mother would say that we had no furniture and no money to buy any. These were small issues as far as I was concerned. All I wanted was to get in there so we could get my brothers and sisters out of the care homes; that was my priority.

I was very frustrated at this situation. Then, one Friday in the winter of 1965 when my mother was at work, there was an unbelievably bad storm, with howling winds and pelting rain. The water came in through the walls at Nan's even more than normal and I was suddenly inspired to take action. My mother was always saying that she was afraid that the house would come down on top of us in bad weather, so I got the sweeping brush and started banging the walls of our room. The whitewash came off in large flakes, creating an off-white carpet on the floor. When my mother came home, I let on to be in an awful state. 'I thought the whole lot would fall on top of me with the storm,' I said, 'we'd better move fast before something terrible happens to us.' She agreed and I was delighted.

Over the next two days, I used an old pram to load and transport our meagre belongings—two chairs, a Formica table, the Singer sewing machine—the twenty-minute walk from Nan's to Ballyseedy. I lugged what I could over the stones that were where the road would later be. A neighbour who had a van transported the two beds to the house. By Sunday, my parents, my two sisters and myself were ensconced in our brand-new home. Nan and Uncle Johnny stayed behind in the old cottage where they remained for a few more years before moving to another house a short distance up the road.

I was so happy to be in the new house; I felt the move to a brand-new home promised a new life for us as a family. It was a semi-detached house and had three bedrooms, a kitchen, a scullery with a tap and running water, a sitting room with a Jubilee range in it, and a little hallway. For the first time in my life, I had a bedroom to myself. Our new neighbours moved in a couple of weeks after us. In total, there were six families, most of them with young children. The strange thing was that my mother would never let my younger siblings mix with the children from the other houses, even though they knew each other from school. She was fearful and wanted to avoid any possible friction so our gate was kept closed at all times and you daren't open it.

I went to work every day and my mother was working a few days a week for the McSweeneys. Finally, my father started to work on a more regular basis. It was still hard to get money off him and my mother would ask me to waylay him on a Friday after he'd been paid to get a few pounds from him before he went into a pub in town. Even though there was very little money coming in, my mother always ensured the rent was paid. She was also buying a few bits and pieces for the house, paying off whatever she could each week. Life was improving; it felt more stable and my parents were getting on better than they had been. I really felt that it was only a matter of time before the other children would be brought home. A few months after the move to the new house, the last member of the family—a boy—was born, in January 1966.

OUR NEW STABILITY was, sadly, short-lived. The stark fact was that neither my mother nor I earned that much, and my father—now that he was earning—was drinking more. He also started beating my mother more regularly when we moved into our new home. I'd seen him hit her before but he hadn't done it so frequently and so violently when we lived at Nan's. One day, after a particularly bad beating, my mother went to Nana Grady's house in Tralee, taking the three small children with her. Nana Grady told her that she couldn't go back to the house while my father was beating her. My mother was at her wits' end and decided to put the three youngest children into care with the older children. For some reason, however, the baby remained with her and they both went from Nana Grady's to the refuge of the County Home in Killarney.

I couldn't believe what was happening; instead of the others coming home, two more of my siblings were now gone into care. I was in despair and even more so when my mother, in a rage, said to me that I must be thrilled that they were gone out of the house. I had been looking after them as much as I could but I was also starting to make a life for myself outside the family home. I had a few friends that I'd talk to after work and I was realising that I deserved a life for myself. When my mother blamed me for the fact that she had to put the girls into the Nazareth, I cried bitter tears and asked her how she could say such a thing. I now know that she just couldn't cope with her situation. I had always been her main support and she could see that I was growing up and would probably soon be gone. The seemingly inevitable happened and the girls spent the next few years in care, not leaving the home until 1970.

For the next two months while my mother and brother remained in the County Home in Killarney, I visited them when I was on my half day from work. I'd take the mid-afternoon train to Killarney and come back on the late-night 'ghost train'. It arrived in Tralee at midnight and, generally, there would be few people on it. One night it was very dark when we pulled into Tralee and I didn't relish the thought of walking all the way out to Ballyseedy alone.

I saw a bike and, without thinking, I got on it and cycled home. Unknown to me, I had been spotted taking the bike and the guards arrived at the house within minutes of me getting there. I was terrified and begged them not to tell my father, saying that he would kill me if he found out. When he heard the commotion, my father came out. The guards could see my fear and told him that if he laid a hand on me, they would arrest him. I had a lucky escape; the guards took the bike and my father didn't hit me.

IT WAS at this time that I experienced poverty in a way I'd never experienced before. I no longer had the back-up of Nan and the support I'd had at her house. Instead, it was just me with my wages and I found it impossible to make ends meet. I needed to visit my mother in Killarney and I'd buy cigarettes for her as they seemed to be the only thing that brought her any comfort. I also visited my siblings in the homes in Tralee and tried to have some small treats for them. On top of all that, I was always trying to give my father something to keep him happy.

Even though we had been brought up with very little, we were always told that we were never, ever to steal; my mother had drummed that lesson into us. But, in the face of the worst deprivation of my life, I started taking cigarettes and money from my employers. Every time I did it, I hated myself and couldn't believe that I was doing something that went against everything I had learned and believed. To lessen my guilt, I kept a list of what I took because I had every intention of paying it all back someday when I'd have enough money in a then-unimaginable future.

Sometime earlier, when I'd come to work one morning and picked up the post in the shop, I saw an envelope with the words CONSCIENCE MONEY written on it. 'It's seldom you get that,' my boss said. 'This is only about the second or third time it has happened.' I asked him what it meant. 'Someone that owed me money felt that they had to give it back. They were ashamed and decided to put it into an envelope and shove it in the door.' That experience stayed with me and, years later, I did the same thing.

I don't think my boss noticed that I was taking any money because I only ever took tiny amounts, or a few cigarettes; either way, he never said that the till was down. Nonetheless, I was terrified that I would be caught. The amount I had taken was growing and I was feeling more and more pressure. I'd always promise myself that the amount wouldn't go over £2, then £3 and so on, but it did and it came to the point where I felt I couldn't cope with the stress anymore. I knew what I was doing was wrong—it was against my principles but I couldn't see any way out of it. In the end, the amount I had taken came to £17, a lot of money when you are only earning £1 a week and responsible for several people.

I came to the point where I knew I just couldn't continue in this way. I had broken the trust that had been put in me by people I loved and I had no way of paying them back. I decided that I had to leave McSweeney's because I could no longer face them even though they didn't know what I had done. I'd have gone immediately only we would have starved; I remember telling my mother I was going to leave my job and she nearly lost her life because the McSweeneys had been so loyal and good to us. I didn't tell her why I wanted to leave; I just said that I was going to get another job.

Some years later, when I had enough saved, I dropped an envelope through McSweeney's letterbox. After that experience, no matter how dire my financial situation was, I never took a penny from anyone. To steal from anyone, not to mention people who trusted me and whom I loved, was totally against who I was and I was determined that, no matter how desperate my life became, I would never put myself in that situation again.

AS ALWAYS, I wanted to make peace and build bridges between my parents. When I visited my mother in Killarney, I'd plead with her to come home again, telling her that my father missed her and was promising that things would change if she came back. Then, when I got home, I'd tell him that she was missing him and wanted to return but that he'd have to change his behaviour. After two months, my efforts worked and my mother came home. I was relieved but also worried, and not without good reason. Within a few months, there was hell in the house again. My father beat my mother badly and she told me that she had to get out; the baby was nervous and she was now afraid for him as well as for herself.

I felt responsible because I'd convinced her that things would be better this time round. I knew she had to go and I also knew that I didn't want to stay in the house alone with my father so I came up with the idea of renting a flat in Tralee. I found a room over a fast-food restaurant in the town and we moved there in September 1967. The woman that owned the flat also lived in the house. It was an awful place; we had one room upstairs with two beds and a table. The one good thing was that we were much nearer the homes where my siblings were and I visited them as often as I could and on Sundays the older boys would come to the flat. I loved to see them and spend time with them. It wasn't possible to bring the girls out so I'd see them in the Nazareth. My mother didn't visit as often. I think she just didn't have the will; she had, in some way, given up from the time she'd first had to let them go.

While we were living in Tralee, I went to work during the day as usual while my mother stayed in the room with the baby. Once the rent was paid and my brother was fed, we had almost no money left for food for ourselves. Things were really horrendous from a financial point of view; I hadn't a penny and once went for two days without eating. I was friendly with a girl who worked as a housekeeper for the local priest and when I visited her, she would always give me a cup of tea. I once saw her throwing food into a bin and came back later and took it out. I knew it wasn't contaminated because she was spotless and had wrapped it up well. If I'd asked her for the leftovers, she would have given them to me; likewise, I could have asked Mrs Mac, but I just couldn't bring myself to ask them for food.

Eventually, I went to my father and asked for help. 'There will be no money handed over here,' he shouted. 'Tell your mother to come home if she wants money.' After that, I would go to Ballyseedy on my half day and plead with him. I was petrified of encouraging my mother to come home again after the last time, but I knew we couldn't afford to stay in Tralee. To placate my father, I would bring him some cigarettes and give him a few shillings that I couldn't afford. When he was more conciliatory, I would try to make him see that what he had done was wrong, and he'd start crying and say that he was sorry. After four months in Tralee, there was no option for us but to return to the house in Ballyseedy, and that is what we did.

ONCE we returned home, there was the usual fragile peace for a while. There was certainly a bit more money available because the council charged a low rent for the house and my father was actually working, so the full financial burden didn't fall on my shoulders. My brothers came out to visit every Sunday. Sometimes they would be in the area on other days, walking in beautiful Ballyseedy Woods with one of the Brothers and the other boys from St Joseph's. I remember running up to them once when I saw them—they couldn't step out of line—and saying hello, delighted to see them and still hoping that the family would be together again one day.

Despite all that had happened in the preceding months, this was, in fact, one of the most positive and memorable years of my life. I've always had the belief that there is something to be salvaged from every situation, that good things are happening around us and that the bad will pass in time. And so, while our domestic horror was taking place in the early part of the year, I met and got to know Seán Hurley, the person who would become my anchor in life, my best friend and my husband.

I had started to socialise a bit with a cousin who was a few years older than me and who lived and worked in Tralee. My mother had no problem giving me permission to go out with her. She brought me to my first hop where Michael Donovan was spinning the records. The girls would stand at one side of the hall with the boys at the other side. There was a bit of a bathroom down at the end; it didn't even have a mirror, which made it difficult for the girls who were anxious to fix their hair and make a good impression.

I had friends for the first time in my life; there was Mary and Dolores who both worked in the presbytery and I also got to know Dermot Crowley who became a great friend. In fact, I really liked Dermot and was hoping he felt the same. We went to the Brass Rail restaurant as often as possible because there was a juke box there. 'The Shoals of Herring', sung by the Clancy Brothers, was a particular favourite of mine and I played it whenever I had a few pennies to spare. We would have soft drinks or tea and chat away to our heart's content. I was there with Dermot on one occasion when he said that he'd like to be introduced to my friend Mary. My jaw dropped. 'My friend Seán fancies you so we could make it a double date,' he added.

I agreed, while trying to hide my disappointment that it wasn't me that Dermot wanted to take out on a date. I had seen and spoken to Seán before and thought he was very handsome. He played music and would come into McSweeney's with other musicians on a Friday evening to have a pint before heading out to play. They were lovely company and I'd be delighted to see them coming in the door.

We went on our first date and straightaway there was a strong and positive connection between Seán and myself. He was a very warm person and it was great to be in the company of someone that I could have fun with. I was only sixteen when we started going out properly in May 1966, but I knew almost immediately that Seán was the man I wanted to marry. That September, when a woman who went to Lourdes every year came in to the travel agency to book her ticket, she said, 'If you have any special intention, write it down, put it in an envelope and I'll bring it to Lourdes for you'. I wrote down my petition: 'If it's God's will, I want to marry Seán.'

I believed it would happen and could even visualise us being married and happy together. In fact, although I didn't know it at the time, Seán and I had met years earlier when we were babies. His family had lived across the street from the house that my parents lived in when they first got married. When our mothers met on the street, Seán and I would smile at each other from our prams, according to my mother.

He was a year older than me and from the Mitchels area in Tralee. Like me, he was the eldest of a large family, seven children in total. His father worked on the railway and his mother worked in their home looking after the children. I could see that he had a very stable family background in comparison to my own. He was the first in his family to receive a scholarship to attend the Christian Brothers-run school known as 'The Green'. When he sat his Inter Cert he came fourth in Ireland in the exam. However, as he was only sixteen, he was deemed too young to go into the senior cycle so he repeated third year and sat the exam again, coming fifth in Ireland this time round.

Following his exams, Seán got a summer job in McCowen's in Tralee. September came round and it was time for him to return to The Green but Seán stalled. There was a Brother there who disliked him and who beat him regularly for no reason at all. Seán told the principal that he wouldn't return if that man was going to be teaching him in the senior years. He was told that the man would, in fact, be one of his class teachers so Seán made the decision not to go back to school. Within two years, the Brother in question left the order and got married. By that stage, Seán was working full time.

McCowen's consisted of a big hardware, foundry and supermarket business and Seán worked in the office which was just down the way from McSweeney's in Castle Street. Our friend Dermot worked there too. Seán was earning £12 a month and he gave his mother a tenner for the family, leaving him with £2 until next payday. He was also playing music with a couple of friends and they might get a fiver between the three of them for a gig. They'd often play three nights a week so he was able to supplement his income substantially in this way.

When Seán and I first started dating, I was allowed out only one night a week—Sunday night—and we would go to the hop where we would meet up with our other friends. The hop was on from half nine until eleven and afterwards Seán would walk me home to Ballyseedy. I started doing my night classes in the technical college the year we began going out so we would meet after class on the Tuesday night as well. I was always dying to hear his band playing and would sometimes tell my parents I was doing an evening shift at the Brass Rail restaurant. Then I'd head off with the lads to wherever they were performing and Seán would give me a few shillings to give my mother as wages from my supposed night's work.

His generosity was far-reaching. From our earliest days together, he was very good to me in every way, including financially. He knew that I had to hand over most of my wages at home and couldn't really afford to go out, much less buy anything for myself, so he bought me the clothes that I needed and wanted. I loved style and if I saw something in Donnelly's in Moyderwell, Seán would buy it for me for my birthday or for Christmas. I loved how warm he was with people; he was very popular and outgoing. He loved music and so did I. He was kind and considerate and he was the first person I'd ever met who didn't make demands of me and who respected me for just being me. Even though I was outgoing, I had this shield in front of me that I didn't let people behind, but with Seán it was different, I could talk to him and he was someone I felt I could really trust.

I had a problem though: I was afraid to open up about what was happening in my family. When I got to know Seán first, my mother, baby brother and I were living in the flat in Tralee. I didn't want to admit we'd had to leave home because of my father's behaviour so I said we were there because he was working in Dingle, adding that we were afraid to stay in the house in the countryside on our own. I was reluctant to tell him that all the rest of my siblings were in St Joseph's and the Nazareth care homes even though my heart was telling me to disclose everything. But I'd grown up in a house where things weren't spoken of or explained; they just were and I'd had to accept every new situation without question, whether I liked it or not.

I hated being caught up in a web of half truths that I knew was undermining my relationship with Seán. I knew he was too important to me and that our connection was too precious to risk losing him by not opening up to him fully. So, gradually, I started telling him about my siblings and where they were living and why we'd had to move into the flat in Tralee.

I told him about how little money we had because my father didn't always work and that, when he did, he more often than not drank or gambled his wages. It was very difficult for me to put words on these experiences but I knew that I had to try. When I finally found the words to articulate what I needed to say, Seán was very understanding and supportive. In fact, he went to the Nazareth at Christmas to play music for the children and he met my sisters there.

One night during the Rose Festival in Tralee, I went to a pub to hear him play music and met his mother and his aunts for the first time. Once that happened, I knew it was time for me to bring him out to Ballyseedy to officially meet my parents. He had already met my father informally in some of the pubs around town where he'd be playing but his coming to the house and meeting my mother was a big moment in my life. I had never brought anyone into the house, not even friends when I was younger, so I was very nervous. I needn't have been; both my parents took to Seán from the moment they met him. My father loved playing cards and so did Seán and we all enjoyed card games together.

On Sundays, he always went for a walk with a friend of his and they'd call into our house in Ballyseedy for a cup of tea around three o'clock. His presence eased the tension that was habitual in our home. When my father would see him coming, he'd say, 'Here comes Long Fella Deeds with his Croke Park ankle' (while playing with the Kerry minors, Seán had gotten an ankle injury). I was happy they were all getting on together; I had always wanted things to be right and now, for the first time ever, it seemed as if there was good reason to hope.

ALTHOUGH I didn't sit the exams at the end of my two-year course at the technical college, I was still chomping at the bit to move on with my work life, especially now that I had a strong relationship with Seán and the promise of a future that offered many possibilities. I still loved working in McSweeney's but I needed to earn more money. I started looking around for other work and, in 1968, I applied for a job at the Pretty Polly hosiery factory in Killarney. I didn't know much about the business except that a huge number of people worked there, including a lot from Tralee, some of whom I knew. They were looking for staff and I decided to give it a go. I had heard about the money they paid and couldn't believe the amount employees were earning. I filled in an application form and was called for an interview. I got the job and went from earning 17 shillings a week to earning £7 a week, getting up to £9 weekly with overtime.

A Pretty Polly bus left Tralee every morning at seven and took all the workers to Killarney where we started work at eight. We would leave the factory at six and be back in Tralee again by seven in the evening. Women's tights were made at the factory and I worked as a seamstress. I'll never forget my first week; the building was huge and I wasn't used to such an environment with so many people and so much noise. It caused me great stress and I began to suffer from violent headaches which continued for as long as I worked there.

I got a headache one day and it was so bad I had to be put into the sick bay. After that, I was moved to a different section where I was sitting nearer a door so that I would have more air. That helped a bit and, over time, I settled in more and got to know a couple of nice people. Overall though, I wasn't happy there. Up until then, I had worked very much on a one-to-one basis with people and now I was working with a machine and felt very isolated despite being surrounded by people. I was very tempted to leave and look for another job but the wages were too good.

SEÁN and I were growing closer and our love for each other was deepening so, in late 1968, we decided to get engaged.

Despite all my troubles with my father, I was still very conservative and explained to Seán that he would have to ask for permission to marry me. On the night we decided that he would ask for my hand, we all went to the Hotel Manhattan just outside Tralee. I remember my hair was in a beehive and I was wearing a dark green and red tartan dress with a little collar and three-quarter length sleeves that were turned up. I advised Seán to buy a few pints for my father to soften him up before he spoke to him. The reaction Seán got when he asked for my hand was 'Take her away, boy, no problem, take her away'. I was delighted.

We went to Cork to get the ring. This was only my second time outside County Kerry; we had travelled to Cork earlier in the year and had gone into a jeweller's shop where Seán had bought me a fob watch because I couldn't wear a watch around my wrist as I had too much static electricity in my body. We returned to the same shop for my engagement ring. It was beautiful, made of pure sapphire and diamonds. It cost £78 which was an absolute fortune in my eyes. Seán had saved up for it with the money he was making from playing in the band. I had never owned anything of such beauty or value in my entire life.

We got officially engaged on All Saints' Day and had a party at the rugby club in Oakpark in Tralee. Seán's family came, though his mother didn't attend because she was heavily pregnant with her youngest child. His father was there, as were both my parents. Our friends attended and Seán's fellow musicians were there also and we had a really enjoyable night.

THROUGHOUT all of the following year we saved hard for the wedding. I gritted my teeth and continued working at Pretty Polly though I couldn't wait to leave. Seán was earning good money at work; he had left McCowen's and was now working for an insurance company and was on a fortnightly wage of £17. There was also a bit more money at home because my father was working more regularly. A man who lived nearby and who had a car called for him each morning to give him a lift to work in Blennerhassett's in Tralee so he had no excuse not to go. My mother still worked in McSweeney's and things at home were on a relatively even keel.

My brothers had come out of St Joseph's when they turned sixteen. I was delighted when this happened though the family reunion I had hoped for didn't materialise. They didn't come to live at home full time because they got jobs in Tralee that had lodgings going with them so they stayed in the town during the week. They came to Ballyseedy at the weekends and were good at giving my mother a bit of money to help her out. In 1969, Joan got out of the Nazareth and came to live at Ballyseedy. She got a job in a shop in Tralee and soon met a boyfriend from Cahersiveen where she spent a good bit of her free time. I loved having her around but we didn't get to see as much of each other as I would have liked because I had to leave the house around six in the morning and wasn't back until after seven at night.

As the wedding day drew closer, I no longer handed all of my wages over to my mother because I needed money for the big day. I had spotted a beautiful dress in Revington's shop in The Mall. It cost £27 and I worked hard to save up for it; eventually I paid £17 while Seán contributed £10. It was a full-length dress with a train and a lace collar and sleeves. I bought material for the bridesmaids' dresses and got them made by a dressmaker. We had set a date for the 13th of June 1970 and I was very happy to hand in my notice at Pretty Polly the month beforehand.

WE GOT married on the day Seán turned twenty-one in Cloghers church in Ballymacelligott parish and had our wedding breakfast in the Grand Hotel in Tralee with about 130 guests attending. Though the custom at the time was for the bride's family to pay for the wedding, we paid for it ourselves, handing over a certain amount on the day and paying the remainder later. Seán's best man was Dermot Crowley, who had introduced us to each other, and his brother Liam was his groomsman. Two of my sisters were my bridesmaids; one of them, who was fifteen at the time, was still in the Nazareth but was allowed out for two days. Seán's sister and another sister of mine, who was also allowed out from the Nazareth, were our flowergirls. My thirteen-year-old sister was brought to the church by the nuns and they took her back to the home after the meal. My brothers were also there and the only siblings who didn't attend were the two youngest.

The night before the wedding I went to McSweeney's to take a bath, a rare luxury. On the morning of the big day, everybody left to go to the church and there was just myself and my father in the house, waiting for the taxi. I was very nervous and wanted a glass of water. Although there were loads of mugs around, I took a cup from the one good set of ware that my mother had which was for display only. The cup slipped out of my hand and smashed into bits on the floor. I became even more nervous then, afraid of what she would say when she found out but I couldn't dwell on it as the taxi driver arrived and it was time to go to the church.

I walked up the aisle with my father. Although he wasn't a good father to me, I had rarely fought with him, having learned early on how to keep out of his way. He got very drunk on the day but, thankfully, he remained sociable. A neighbour brought him home that night about eight o'clock and there was a sense of relief when he was gone because my mother could enjoy herself then. Nan was at the wedding, as were my Uncle Johnny and all the neighbours. It was a lovely day and wonderful to have so many of the family together for the first time. For our honeymoon, we went on a train journey to the southeast, staying first at the Sunset Ridge Hotel in Cork and travelling from there to Waterford.

We had rented a flat near Basin View in Tralee. It had a bedroom, kitchen, living room and a bathroom. My mother gave us a sideboard which she had paid for by the week and Seán's mother gave us two fireside chairs. In those days people used give a lot of practical wedding presents—kettles, ware, cutlery and sheets—which was very handy. When we returned from our honeymoon, I couldn't wait to go in the door of our new home. I felt that a new and exciting chapter in my life had begun.

CHAPTER THREE

NEW BEGINNINGS

O NCE we had unpacked, I travelled to Ballyseedy to visit my parents. When I went into the house I was absolutely shocked to see that all my siblings were now out of care. It was a Sunday and they were all sitting together around the table, eating dinner. My four younger sisters had joined my parents, my other sister and the youngest boy at home, while the two older boys were there at weekends. This is what I had always wanted—everybody to be at home—but it had happened immediately after I had left the house forever.

I was taken aback and angry; I asked my mother why this couldn't have happened earlier. She explained that she'd had to wait for paperwork to be processed and that she hadn't done it deliberately. I was destined never to live under the same roof as the entire family again and this caused me much sadness. But I accepted the situation and focused on the positive; the family was together again and I would be able to visit them; also, I was happily married to a man I loved dearly and was looking forward to starting my own family.

My older siblings were all set up in jobs fairly quickly as the Sisters and Brothers made sure that those who passed through their hands were schooled and trained in useful trades and skills. They told me of the tough times they had gone through and how hard it was sometimes to maintain hope that they would ever get out of care. While they were happy to be back living with my parents, life—unsurprisingly—wasn't easy. The older ones helped out financially but my father's physical abuse of my mother continued and intensified over the following years, and he also beat some of my siblings.

I visited generally on a Sunday when, for whatever reason, my father was always on his best behaviour so I didn't witness any of his violent outbursts and only heard about them afterwards. We never confronted him about how he treated us as a family and as individuals, maybe because we felt it would make our mother's life more difficult and we loved her so much that was the last thing we would have wanted to do. There is no doubt he made all our lives much more difficult than they needed to be, but we tapped into the resilience that we had inherited from Nan and our mother to survive the dark times.

SEÁN and I settled in very happily to married life in Basin View. I loved the freedom of being in my own home and of not having anybody to answer to or look after except Seán and myself. This was soon to change, however, because I was pregnant with our first child. I had always wanted a family of my own to cherish and protect and I couldn't wait for our first baby to be born. Seán was working full time with an insurance company and playing music so—for the first time in my life—I wasn't working. Liam was born in 1971 and we were over the moon; we were now a complete family.

As the baby got bigger, I found it difficult to get in and out of the flat with a pram so when an apartment came up for rent in Denny Street we took it. Now we were right in the centre of town and I enjoyed being able to get around more easily. I visited Ballyseedy on a regular basis, always on a Sunday with Seán and maybe once during the week when I'd get a taxi there. Life was good; I'd had very little freedom when was younger so I loved to go out socially. One of my brothers was working in Benner's Hotel and if he was off he would babysit of a night and I'd go to hear Seán and the band play at The Parklands, or we would go to the Abbey Inn to play cards, which we both loved.

When Liam was eight months old, the John Mitchels team organised a tour to America. Seán, as a team player, was going and as all the wives were going too, he wanted me to join him. I wasn't sure what to do as the trip was three weeks long and it wasn't possible to take the baby. In the end, I said I would go and my mother agreed to look after Liam. I had never been abroad before; in fact, Cork and Waterford were still the only places outside County Kerry I had been to.

I was very excited at the thought of going to the States with a great bunch of people. We went to Chicago, Philadelphia and New York where the players were welcomed like royalty. It was a great trip but I was upset at leaving the baby behind and missed him terribly, even when I was enjoying myself. I also had a miscarriage while I was there which was very upsetting. I was relieved to return home and soon after I was pregnant again. Our second son, Seánie, was born in April 1973.

SHORTLY after we got married in 1970, we had applied to the council for a house. There were houses being built in Hawley Park and we were told that we would get one of those when they were completed. The system was that you could rent or buy the house from the council. Rent was about £1 per week and if you were buying you had to pay £5.34 a week, which was a lot of money at the time. We decided to buy even though everyone thought we were mad. My thinking was that the rent would inevitably go up and if we owned the house we would have a chance later on of selling it and moving out to the countryside which is where we wanted to bring up our family. Farmers' Bridge, where Nan was originally from, was where both Seán and I had in mind from our earliest married days, even when we had very little money.

I was twenty-four when we moved into Hawley Park. This was the first home that we owned and it was a brand-new house. There was an upstairs bathroom, three bedrooms—two upstairs and one downstairs—as well as a living room, sitting room and kitchen. The neighbours were lovely and I was really enjoying motherhood and, in 1975, our third son, Pat, was born.

Because we were paying to buy the house, money was tighter than it had been when we had been renting, so I started to think of ways I could supplement our income. The first thing I did was take in two tenants on a bed-and-board basis. There were AnCO students and would stay with us from Sunday night until Friday. I was getting £7 a week from them; it was a nice little bit of money and I did that for a year or so. The group Seán played with—the Hamilton Folk Group—was in great demand. They would play up to five nights a week. There was a huge upsurge in interest in ballad singing at that time and they got gigs in lots of towns around the county. Any opportunity I got, I would go and listen to them. My main social outlet, though, was bingo on a Friday or Sunday night. It was on mostly in Horan's and I absolutely loved going there when I could.

By 1976, we needed additional steady income, what with the cost of the house and a growing family, so I got a job in St Catherine's Hospital. It was tough going; the shifts were from nine at night until nine in the morning, seven days on, seven days off. My duties included working on reception, answering the phone and the doors, doing the cleaning, bringing drinks to the patients and alerting the necessary medical people when there were emergency calls. While working at the hospital, I became pregnant with our first daughter, Mairead, who was born in November 1977.

Having four young children, a job and a husband who worked full time during the day and on many nights had to take its toll, and it did. Although we were young and healthy, our work-life balance was tilting out of sync and the result was that I became quite ill. I was so busy I didn't even notice at first. One morning I came home and all four children were sick. I called the doctor who took one look at me and told me I had pneumonia. I knew then I couldn't keep up with the night shifts and trying to get the kids up and out to school and nursery pre-school in the mornings. Something had to give so I gave up St Catherine's.

Once we all recovered, I was full of energy again and got a job with Dunnes Stores in 1978. The hours were more suitable for someone with a young family and I enjoyed working there, mixing with the customers and getting to meet with other adults during the day. I was responsible for the fruit and vegetables and ensuring they were brought into the shop and shelved. If it was very busy, I would go on the tills. I would bring the older children in with me before they went to school when I was on the early shift and I would finish around two or three o'clock.

I was on a different rota every week and arranging the minding of the smaller ones was difficult, but between Seán and myself we managed it. Sometimes I would get one of my sisters or brothers to mind the children but that wasn't too often because my mother didn't approve for fear something would happen them. I didn't understand it but that was her way. Then I became pregnant again and our son Brian was born in 1979.

It was high time to get a car which we did around this time. Our first purchase was a Morris Minor. I didn't know how to drive and, foolishly, assumed it was like riding a bicycle so I got into the car and drove to my mother's with the children. I had to get a neighbour to reverse it for me and turn it in the direction of Tralee. Then I had to get one of the children to go to the end of the road to see if there were any cars on the main road. I made sure I got driving lessons after that!

SEÁN and I had a very busy family and work life but we also had a five-year plan to move from Hawley Park to Farmers' Bridge so that the children could be brought up in the freedom of the countryside. People thought we were mad, just as they had when we said we were buying the house in Hawley Park from the council. Now they couldn't understand why we wanted to leave a perfectly good home and go to the trouble of building a brand-new house. But it was our dream and by the late 1970s it started to appear in bricks and mortar.

Seán was earning a good wage at PMPA Insurance and we were able to get a loan from them. This allowed us to buy a site from an uncle of mine for £500 and to get a mortgage. We sold the house in Hawley Park for £10,500. We paid £2,500—our outstanding payments— to the council and were able to put the remaining money towards the building of our new home. I bought a book of sample houses and we chose a design from that. A relation worked on the plans and we applied for planning permission. It cost £17,000 to build the new house which was completed within twelve months.

We moved to Farmers' Bridge in 1979. It was fantastic to have so much space for our growing family and to be back in the beautiful countryside and near to where I had grown up. Nan, sadly, had died a few years earlier and I missed not having her nearby but I always remembered her with great affection and love. Uncle Johnny still lived in the area and, of course, my parents were just down the road at Ballyseedy. I was now thirty and felt I had come a long way in the ten years since I had walked out the door of my parents' house to get married.

I was looking forward to spending more time with my mother now that we were living close to each other but that wasn't to be. Shortly after we moved out to Farmers' Bridge, my parents moved into Hawley Park. My sister Joan lived at 38 Hawley Park with her husband and children (we had lived at number 13) and she and my parents did a swop. Joan loved the countryside and my parents, who didn't have a car and were getting older, felt they would be better off living in the town with all the facilities nearby. I was very disappointed with the move because I had wanted to be near my mother. After moving to Hawley Park, even though she had really wanted to go there, my mother was not happy. Basically, she was a country woman at heart.

FOR OUR first few years at Farmers' Bridge, we had a relatively comfortable life with Seán working by day and night and earning good money. With five children, I had plenty to keep me busy but, as ever, I wanted to earn some money and contribute to the household. Although we were in a rural area, it was fairly populated and I came up with the idea of opening a small shop in the house where I could sell basic groceries. I would work from home and that would be very handy. We converted a room off the kitchen into a shop and opened for business within a few months of moving in. It cost about £800 for the conversion and the stock and I was delighted with myself. There was a big fridge for milk, cheese, ham and cold drinks. I also sold bread, milk, cigarettes, sweets, gravy, tomato ketchup and washing powder—all the staples of a country shop. If someone asked me for something and we didn't have it, I would get it the following day.

It was my first time being self-employed and I made a hames of it. There was no such thing as stock control or checking the money; I just kept buying. We sold ham and more of that ended up on our own kitchen table than was bought; the kids had it for breakfast, dinner and supper. I used go out one night a week to play cards and, before I would leave the house, I'd hide the shop door key. I didn't realise that the older boys were keeping a tight eye on me to see where I was putting it. I was no sooner gone than they were into the shop and eating whatever sweets they could get their hands on. I did notice that they were often sickish on Mondays but I didn't link it to their secret sweet feasts. I only found out what they were up to when there was a fight among the boys and one of them spilled the beans.

This was a wake-up call for me. I stood back and looked at the bigger picture. There were several problems: we were all eating from the shop without paying; the customer base was small; I was inexperienced and had made lots of mistakes. Also, I was now finding the work monotonous and tiring. The shop was open from early morning until ten at night (eight on a Sunday). I remember on Christmas night in 1980 when someone came to the door at half past twelve looking for cigarettes. I had a decision to make: re-commit to the shop and do it properly or close it and look for something that paid more and that I liked more. I took the latter option and closed the door of Hurley's Shop in 1981 after almost two years in business.

1981 WAS a time of work change for Seán too. He had been working in the insurance business for many years as an employee and was very popular with clients. He made the decision to go out on his own and set up his own brokerage. For this he needed about £400 which we borrowed from the credit union. He was enthusiastic about his new endeavour but soon found that it was very difficult as a new broker to get the most competitive quotes for clients. He saw fairly quickly that he was running into difficulty and got a job again, this time with a company based in Cavan.

He was paid on commission and had a lot of travelling to do and it was soon obvious that it wasn't going to work out financially. Luckily, he was still playing music—the band now played at weddings as well—so there was some money coming into the house. It wasn't enough, however, and I decided to try and get a full-time job. That would mean Seán could mind the kids during the day and I would be home in the evening so he would be free to play music when the band had gigs.

A few people I knew, including a good friend of mine, a cousin and my sister Miriam's husband, were all working at a factory in Tralee called WABCO Westinghouse. The conditions were good and so were the wages. They manufactured signal lights for railways and I got a job there in 1981 on the assembly line. I worked a split shift—six to two and two to ten. Unlike my earlier factory experience, in Pretty Polly, I enjoyed my time there and made many good friends. With Seán at home minding the kids, life was much easier. I got pregnant with our son Martin while I was there and he was born in 1982. I returned to work after the birth, although that was hard with the split shifts.

As we only had one car, Seán would collect me when I was finished work. One night I got a call saying that there had been a car accident and that Seán wouldn't make it in. I was frantic with worry and got a lift home from my friend's husband. There was a very bad storm that night and our car had become stuck in a flood. Seán was uninjured but the fire brigade had to be called to get him to safety. He later wrote a funny song about the incident but it wasn't funny when we realised that we now had no car and no money to get another one.

I finally had to face a truth that I had managed to avoid dealing with for a while. In the midst of the happiness, joy, chaos, busyness and hard work that was our life, I had noticed some years earlier that Seán was drinking too much. The nature of the work he was doing by night—playing music in bars and hotels—meant that fans would buy drinks for the band members and line them up in front of them. I always knew he liked a few pints but, after he left his insurance job, his dependency on alcohol grew as the disease took a greater hold of him.

He was still a wonderful husband and father, with the same warm and supportive personality he had always had. However, we now had six children and not enough money to support ourselves. Losing the car made me realise that working from home, if I could find a business that was sustainable, would be our best option. I left WABCO in 1983 with no concrete plan in mind other than I wanted and needed to work for myself from home.

I HAD always been good at baking, a skill I inherited from my mother who made the most delicious brown bread, so I decided I would start a homebaking business, supplying a small number of shops. I liked the idea of being able to work from home, of spending more time with the children and of being my own boss. And I also loved baking which was a real plus. I got a few clients pretty easily and was soon busy making squares of bread, apple tarts and a variety of scones. The kids helped out after school, peeling and cutting up apples and making the dough with me.

I did the deliveries myself as well. I would take the kids to school in the morning with all the baking carefully covered in the boot of the car. I enjoyed the homebaking because I knew I was good at it. People liked my produce and would compliment me on it and I liked that. It was great; I was creating something people liked and was getting paid for it.

Then I started getting more and more orders and this proved challenging. My main problem was that I only had a domestic-size oven and there was no way I could fulfil the number of orders coming in. One day I got an order for eight apple tarts and there wasn't a hope I could do it as I also had brown bread and scones to make. Without another oven, I couldn't keep up the required rate of production. I hadn't expected my baking enterprise to take off so quickly and I wasn't ready to expand. I soon saw that I hadn't planned this well at all. I even went down the road to my sister's house to use her oven sometimes, but that was, ultimately, impractical.

I knew I was out of my depth when I got an electricity bill for £700; it floored me. I hadn't thought about how much that bill was going to be. I had the product and the customers but I had no idea how much it was costing me to create and deliver my produce. Once the bill came in, I knew I had to stop. I hadn't enough money to pay it, and to make more money I would have to sell more produce and use more electricity. I was caught in that bind that so many people find themselves in when they first start out in business.

I wanted to stay working from home and came up with the ingenious idea of creating food that needed little or no electricity: salads. It was summertime and I started making coleslaw. In the early 1980s, coleslaw was new and growing in popularity. I also made potato salad. The same shops that had taken my baking now took the salads. I was about three weeks into it when I was asked if I made Waldorf salad. 'Yes,' I replied before rushing to Joan's house to consult one of her recipe books. I had never heard of Waldorf salad before. I read the recipe and went off and bought the ingredients and had it ready for the following morning. But it was very expensive to make and I didn't offer to make it again.

I had learned my lesson with the electricity bill and wasn't about to be caught with Waldorf salads that might have tasted good but weren't that much in demand in Tralee. As the end of the summer of 1983 came round, the end of the salad season arrived as well. Back then, Irish people didn't eat salads outside of the summer months, so once autumn arrived, it brought with it the end of my second food enterprise within a twelve-month period.

WHILE I was doing my baking and salad making, Seán had found a job with Slattery's travel company, who had a bus and coach depot near where we lived. They also had horse-drawn caravans that tourists would hire during the summertime. Their business was getting busier and one day Seán said that they needed help cleaning the inside of the buses that came into the depot each day. We approached them to see if they wanted regular cleaners. They did so I started cleaning buses shortly after finishing my homebaking enterprise.

It was a busy job. The buses would come in late at night and early in the morning. Many of them were coming from or going to London and they were on the road every day of the week. It was the cheapest way to travel at the time and the buses travelled to Victoria Station in London, picking up passengers at certain towns and cities along the way. Once the buses arrived at the depot, they needed to be turned around fairly quickly.

They were fifty-two-seater buses and we would have to clean the windows, the seats and the floors, as well as the ashtrays. In those days, smoking wasn't yet banned and the ashtrays would be overflowing with butts. Nevertheless, the work suited me; it was just over the road from the house and only a few minutes away. The kids would be in bed at night when the buses came in and we would run over and get them done. They were gone to school by day and when they got home I would be around again, having already cleaned the buses that had come in during the middle of the day, so it was very convenient.

The pay was average; we got £3 a bus. Then I found out about buses that were at the Brandon Hotel in Tralee. These were tour buses carrying tourists who were staying overnight in the hotel. One evening I called into the parking area and approached one of the bus drivers who was cleaning his bus. 'I could do that for you,' I said. The drivers were already well paid and were happy to pass the cleaning work over to me. The buses were owned by different operators and it was the bus drivers themselves who paid me. We got £10 per bus, a significant increase on what we were getting for cleaning the other buses. We often had about ten buses to clean in an evening. Seán and some of our children would come in with me to help out. This was good work but, as it was seasonal, we continued with the other bus cleaning as well.

LIFE was busy; our son Conor was born in 1986 so now there were seven kids ranging in age from fifteen down. It could be chaotic at times but we always pulled together as a family, and even when the children were very young they were willing to help out. Naturally enough, there had to be a treat or some payment at the end of the job! Most of them were in school by now in Tralee. When we moved to Farmers' Bridge, they had gone to my former national school at Caherleaheen but Seán and I decided to move them to national school in the town because of an incident where they had been dropped to the school and it didn't open. The children were left standing outside and nobody contacted either Seán or myself and they were freezing by the time we picked them up. We decided then it would be handier all round if they all went to Tralee as the older children were already attending secondary there.

I had always liked being busy and now, with the bus cleaning work and the family, I was very, very busy. However, I was still nurturing the notion of having my own business and of being my own boss. From as far back as I could remember, I had always wanted to work for myself. I had never forgotten the day when I was fourteen years old and was babysitting one of my younger siblings;

I held the child high in the air and declared to her, 'One day I will be my own boss. I will have my own business and house where I will bring children who have nowhere to go and I will take care of them'.

I was surprised at what I had said but the memory of that moment and the absolute conviction that what I had said was true had stayed with me. I had really enjoyed the buzz I got from my homebaking business in 1983; the fact that I was on the first step of the learning ladder then meant that I made many mistakes but that didn't put me off dreaming while I was working on the buses about what I could do next.

I've always been a firm believer in talking to people and making personal connections; it's something that comes very naturally to most Irish people and I certainly was a talker. Also, face-to-face communication was the main way we had in the 1980s of sharing news and information. A friend of mine, Maureen, who had been running a thriving newsagency in Tralee for several years, told me she was thinking of retiring and that the lease would be coming up for renewal. 'Why don't you apply for it?' she said. I had spoken to her on several occasions previously about my desire to have a business of my own so we talked seriously about this proposition. The shop was on the same street—Castle Street—as McSweeney's, where I had cut my teeth behind a counter. I'd had four years of working in every aspect of that business, and had not only been a willing employee while I was there, but I had also really loved dealing with the public. I did have some reservations, though; the hours were long—from seven in the morning until eleven at night, seven days a week. However, after talking it over with Seán, we decided to go for it.

In 1987, I approached the letting agents and we agreed a price on an initial lease of two years and eleven months. I knew it was a big commitment but I was delighted when everything was signed and we could start getting ready to open up Healy's Dairy, as the business had long been known. It was a typical newsagent's with a grocery attached—the forerunner of today's convenience stores. We sold newspapers, baked produce, milk, butter, confectionary and general groceries. People came in early in the morning for their paper and some groceries and we would have the schoolchildren in during their lunch break and after school. There was also a steady stream of customers during the day. There would be another surge in the late evening when people were making their way home from work. I had done the baking and the buses but this was my first real business and I loved it; the work at Healy's Dairy was very much up my alley.

Seán and I did split shifts in the shop; I'd do the early shift and he would go in at three o'clock so I was at home when the kids came in from school to give them their dinner. I would go back then at seven and close up each night at eleven. We only had one car so I would drop Seán in for the morning shift before returning home to get the kids ready for school. Then I would drive back into Tralee with them. Trying to create a workable schedule was difficult but we managed it and, over the months, we started to build up a good business. I loved the buzz of it all. I'll always remember the Rose Festival in our first year—there were huge crowds of people in the streets and we were so busy we had to close the shop at one stage to restock it.

When you are dealing with the public there will always be drama and the events of one particular morning in Healy's Dairy have gone down in our family history. I used to stock delicious apple tarts made by a local woman (who was doing what I had been doing some years earlier) and the morning's delivery had just been made. I put the six tarts on the counter and attended to a customer. When she left the shop, I noticed that one of the tarts was missing. She was the first person in since I had put them on the counter so I knew she must have stolen a tart. I grabbed the sweeping brush and ran out the door and down the street after her. She was holding the stolen tart and I gave it a tip with the brush and knocked it out of her hand. There was no way I was going to let her keep it without paying for it! All this was witnessed by the owner of the bar across the road. She was a tough old woman but she shouted across to me, 'By God, I wouldn't like to cross you!'.

Things were going well in the shop but Seán and I barely saw each other between the split shifts and his music playing at weekends. It was non-stop ferrying the kids in and out to Tralee to school. They would come to the shop before and afterwards and the older ones were great to do a shift as well. On Saturday mornings, the two oldest worked there which meant Seán and I could be at home together for some bit of time with the others. I knew running the shop would be like walking a tightrope but, increasingly, life began to feel like a juggling game with too many balls to be kept in the air.

After a while, I noticed that things weren't going as well as they had been in the business. The recession of the 1980s was kicking in but there was also another issue. Seán's problem with alcohol had come to the fore again. At the time I was so busy I didn't see this happening, but eventually realised it was having an impact on our working lives. We rented a small house near Healy's Dairy in the hope that if we were based in Tralee and didn't have so much driving to do each day, we'd be able to focus more on the business.

That eased things a bit in terms of the daily schedule— the kids could walk to school now and I was just beside the shop. It was then, however, that I made what I will always consider to be one of my biggest business mistakes: I took over the operation of a small fast-food outlet. A friend of mine was running the Rock Grill in Rock Street and she had to go to hospital for an operation. I said that I would cover while she was away; there was no lease or anything like that but I had to buy stock and pay whatever bills arose while I was there.

Healy's Dairy wasn't going well at that point and I thought this new venture might help keep our heads above water. I took over around the time of the Rose Festival which, of course, was a good week, but after that it very quickly became apparent that this was not going to work. There was no way I could run both businesses, and neither was going well enough to justify taking on an employee. I was depending on Seán and the older children to help out but they were at school during the day and my husband was in the grip of a disease that he was struggling to deal with. I knew almost immediately that the situation wasn't viable and that something had to give. I was the juggler trying to keep all the balls in the air and I was failing; they were dropping all round me. One day, I closed the door of the Rock Grill and walked away from it knowing that I wouldn't be opening it ever again, even though I owed money to suppliers.

I STARTED attending Al-Anon during this period. I didn't want to go but a cousin that I was very close to recommended it. 'But I don't have a problem with drink,' I said to her. She explained that the group was for those who live with people with a drink problem. I agreed to go to a meeting thinking there would be a quick-fix solution but, of course, there wasn't. I spoke to someone there and they encouraged me to attend six meetings and to decide then whether I wanted to continue or not.

During those meetings I learned all about the 12-step programme; it is the same structure as the AA programme except it's for the families of those who are drinking excessively. The programme teaches you how to focus on yourself and not on the person who is drinking. It also teaches you that alcoholism is a disease and should be treated as such and that we shouldn't blame a person for having this disease.

I became a calmer person and stopped wasting time arguing with Seán. Al-Anon changed me for the better and helped me learn to focus on myself and on my reactions. Once I learned to react differently to the disease I found that Seán's drinking didn't upset me as much. It taught me that I needed to ensure that I had a separate life for myself outside of the person with the disease, which is so very important because this is a disease which can consume family life if it is allowed to. I started to look after myself a bit more, taking time for something as simple as a walk or a rest. I learned that, step by step, we all need to take ownership of our life. Al-Anon literally saved me; it was a great support and I use the book I got back then right up to the present day because there is a relevant message in it for every day no matter what situation we are in.

HEALY'S DAIRY was still on a downward spiral, with bills mounting and business decreasing. I went to the credit union to apply for a loan to pay for the newspapers and the VAT. I didn't want to have to do that and knew that I was in serious financial trouble when I had to resort to getting loans to pay off bills for produce already sold. I didn't talk to anyone about the sea of problems in which I was now drowning; I didn't ask my family or anyone else for help. Pride kept me silent and I prayed that no one would know how badly off we really were.

In the autumn of 1989, a day dawned when I knew there was no other option but to hand the keys back. It broke my heart to have to give up on the shop but I knew there was no way I could bring it back to where it needed to be. I went to the letting agents to tell them that I had to give up the lease before the full term. I cried because I felt I had, somehow, broken their trust in me. They could have taken a different tenant but they had trusted me and given me the lease and now, here I was, telling them that I had failed. The agent was kind to me and said he would try and get someone in quickly so that there wouldn't be any penalties imposed on me. Within a month or so, they had secured a new tenant.

WHEN I walked in the door of our home after handing back the keys of Healy's Dairy, I wanted to lock myself away and never again go outside. In my mind, everything had gone wrong and I had no idea how we were going to survive. At a practical level, we had hardly any money coming in; Seán was still playing music but he was also drinking heavily. We had seven children ranging in age from eighteen down to three who needed to be fed and educated. I owed money to suppliers from both the Rock Grill and Healy's Dairy. These were people who had trusted me and I felt terrible that I had broken that trust.

I owed VAT and our home bills had also been mounting; the electricity and phone bills remained unopened and we were way behind with our mortgage payments. I couldn't open the post; the bills kept coming in but I never opened them. There was no point as there was no money to pay any of them. When the phone rang, I would put on a strange voice and say, 'No, she's not here'. In those final months before closing Healy's Dairy, we had only been making enough money to put food on the table. The reality was, with the huge number of hours that had to be put in daily, along with the recession, the business was always going to be a massive challenge.

We were on the breadline and it was like being in a deep hole; everything had gone wrong. At least the children's allowance was a help. It meant that we always had something to eat, even if it was porridge twice a day. But we didn't have any money to pay our mounting bills or the mortgage so I went to the welfare office and asked for help. The officer gave me money and I was mortified. I just couldn't handle being back in the poverty trap again.

As bad if not worse than the fact that we were in a terrible financial situation was the shame that was consuming me. I didn't want to meet anyone and I didn't want anyone to see me. I only went into town when I couldn't get out of having to go there; I would drop the kids to school and drive back home immediately. In fact, there were many days when there was no money to buy petrol and if they didn't get a drive, the children would have to walk the three miles into town to school, a journey I had often made myself in my youth.

Nobody knew how desperate our situation was. When asked why we had closed the shop, I would say that the hours were terrible and that the children were too young and needed me at home. I would tell them anything bar the full truth. I became very depressed and just before Christmas of 1989 I reached the lowest point in my life.

I had faced many challenges and difficult situations before but, somehow, this time, a blackness came over me and I could see no way out. One day I was in the car, not far from the house, feeling desperate as I did every day now. There was a wall in front of me and I thought that if I crashed into it, everything would be over and this pain would stop. But the thought of the children pulled me back and, within moments, I shook myself out of that mindset. I knew I had to tackle this and went to the doctor who prescribed anti-depressants.

THAT CHRISTMAS was bleak even though we did have a bit of money coming in. Seán was still earning from playing music and he was back on track health-wise, and we also had the children's allowance. We knew that we weren't going to get support from any bank; we were facing into our third year in arrears with our mortgage and at one point we were around £3,000 in debt for that alone. Even though I wasn't opening the bills, I knew what was in them. You think if you don't open them they will go away, but they don't. I knew that we needed to do something radical.

In February 1990, Seán went to England to find work. He secured a job by March and our son Liam joined him in June. Seánie went over to his father and brother shortly after that. The two boys were both talented musicians and wanted to spread their wings and earn some money, away from recession-ridden rural Ireland. All three sent money home to me to help run the house and feed the children. I also got a part-time job in a supermarket in Tralee where I worked five days a week. I was a very good worker so the owner let me work around the children's school hours.

We got back on to a bit of a level keel again with the two boys and Seán working in England and sending money home. Things were still very tight and we weren't able to pay off any of the bills, but at least there appeared to be a glimmer of light on the horizon. Then Seán had an accident at the builders' providers where he worked. His foot was broken when something fell on it. There was no way he could keeping working in the short to medium term and so he returned to Ireland. Now our main income stream was gone again.

It felt as if the world was conspiring against us. On top of that, I was still severely ashamed that we owed so much money locally and to the banks. I knew at this stage that we were in danger of losing the house. I couldn't bear the thought of having to depend on the State to put a roof over our heads as had happened with my parents. I had moved away from the poverty and hunger of my youth yet here it was again, staring me straight in the face.

I had risen to the many challenges in my life and I had always survived; I had always found a solution but this time I couldn't see a solution in Ireland, only walls closing in all around us no matter where we turned. I could feel the pressure mounting as my stress levels got higher and my blood pressure shot through the roof. I needed a break and to get away from the strain of opening the door and having to meet people and pretend everything was okay. If I had a bit of headspace, I knew that I would be able to think clearly again and come up with a plan, and we badly needed a plan at that stage. I decided that I would go over to London for a week so I rang my sister Miriam and asked her if I could visit. That was no problem, she said. My mind was made up: I was going to London and I wasn't coming back without a plan even though I had no idea what that plan might be. I was heading into unchartered territory.

CHAPTER FOUR

LEAPING INTO
THE UNKNOWN

I HAD to wait until family allowance day—a Tuesday—to get money to buy the ticket for the journey to London. The following day I got on a Slattery's bus, one of those that I had cleaned years earlier, and set off to find a solution to the situation we were in. It was late August, the last days of a beautiful summer that had been one of the most stressful of my forty years. There were many firsts for me that day: it was my first time travelling alone; my first time being away from my children overnight since twenty years earlier when I had gone to America and left our firstborn with my mother; my first time going to London. It was also the first time in my life that I didn't have a plan. I had no idea what the future held; I only knew that I had to do something.

Although I was lonely to be leaving the kids behind, once the bus moved off, my overwhelming feeling was one of relief that I was finally doing something, that I was taking action. I instinctively felt that the mere act of getting away from where all the problems were would help me gain perspective and allow me see that there was a bigger picture; that our lives were, in fact, bigger than the stress and unhappiness that was dominating us. I didn't really know what I was going to do, but I felt that, once I got to London, I would find a way.

I didn't take a cabin on the boat and tried instead to sleep on my bus seat. It was a long journey; we left Tralee at one o'clock in the afternoon and didn't get into Victoria Station until seven o'clock the following morning—a nineteen-hour journey—and I was exhausted by the time we arrived in London. When I got off the bus I was overwhelmed by the tall buildings and the smell of smog. I had little experience of cities and had only been to Cork twice before arriving in London.

Then I discovered that I had lost the piece of paper I had with the directions to Miriam's house written on it. I began to panic. I knew her address, Barnet in north London, but I hadn't a clue how to get there. I had to use the Underground but I had no idea which line to get. I felt overwhelmed and was scared stiff. Eventually, I spotted someone wearing a uniform and approached them. In the end—and it seemed endless—I found myself on the right line. I finally emerged from the Underground onto the street in north Barnet. I spotted a phone booth and called Miriam. She worked as an operator in a cab office and arranged for a cab to collect me. I was never as happy to see her as I was that day. It was three o'clock by the time I got to her house, having stepped off the bus in Victoria Station at seven that morning. It had taken me eight hours to complete what was normally a journey of less than one hour.

My sister was living with her husband, who was from Northern Ireland and worked in the Underground, and their two children. She had been great to my two sons and Seán when they'd arrived in London earlier in the year and she extended that generosity to me as well. As soon as I had called home to let them know I had arrived safely, I told Miriam my story and I didn't hold back. I really felt this was my time to start anew and it could only be done if I was totally open and honest about the situation we were in. She assured me that I'd be fine and I agreed, too tired not to, before going to bed and falling into an exhausted sleep.

MIRIAM finished her shift at three o'clock, so, the next day after work she and I went for a walk around the area. The first thing I noticed was the huge number of ads in shop windows advertising jobs. I was amazed; there were no jobs in Ireland at the time and to walk down a street and see so much opportunity was unbelievable. I wrote down all the contact numbers of those looking for cleaners, bar workers and shop assistants. I knew then that this was a place of opportunity. Here I am, I thought, and here I am staying. I knew I wasn't going to go back to what I had at home. It didn't matter what job I got; all I wanted was to do well-paid work so that we would have a solid foundation again. I couldn't do this in Ireland but London offered prospects I could only have dreamed of.

That evening I went through my list and started making phone calls. I had written down about twenty numbers so if one didn't answer it didn't matter, I would just phone the next one. I called a company called Superdrug who were about to open a store in the area. They asked me to come in for an interview, which I did, and they offered me a job stocking shelves. They didn't ask how long I was in London or what my plans were; all they wanted to know was if I had experience in retail, which I had, and I started work on the following Monday morning. I had planned on staying in London for a week only, but now, having secured work so easily, I decided to go with the flow.

I rang Seán and told him I had taken a job for a week. 'Are you mad?' he asked. 'I am,' I said, 'but that is me.' He had thought I was only going away for a week's break; he had no idea that I might look for a job or consider working full time in London. Because I had been burning our bills, he didn't know the full extent of how desperate our financial situation was but I did and I knew we just had to have some kind of secure, regular income.

Without over-thinking things, I started at Superdrug, which is very similar to Boots. I worked like a Trojan that first week, from early morning until ten o'clock at night, to get the store ready for its official opening. On the Friday when all the shelves were fully stocked they started training people on the tills and I was trained as well. The shop opened for business on Saturday and when I arrived at work it got so busy I was put on the tills straightaway. I was shaking for fear I would make a mistake; everything was computerised and while I had a lot of retail experience, I'd never worked a payment system as sophisticated as this. But I was super-fast and they left me on the tills all day.

My initial notion was that I would work for a week, get some money and then decide what to do. I was due to be paid on the Friday but that was delayed until the following Monday. By the time Monday arrived, I was already rostered for work for the following week so I decided to stay on. I was earning £7 an hour and had done a huge number of hours that first week so when I got paid, I got a nice amount. I gave Miriam a bit for my bed and board and put the rest aside. It was a great feeling to earn money and have it in my pocket. But the real plus was that I was free; nobody knew me and I wasn't trying to hide or explain myself to anybody.

I rang Seán at home and broached the subject of staying in London. I thought it would be a good idea, I explained, if I stayed on for a while to make some money. He listened to what I was proposing, knowing how low I had been before I left for London, how I didn't want to go out or answer the door or the phone. I said that we could see how things went for a few weeks and that, if I could get more work and secure a house, we could all move over to London for a while. He said we should think about it and see if it was workable. Once I had spoken to him, a plan began to formulate in my mind: I would get more work and I would work as hard as I could to save so that I could rent a house and pay to bring the entire family over to London. I could see it all so clearly; the week away had cleared the fog that had been clouding my thinking and I could, finally, see a way forward that would benefit us all.

In the end, the decision to stay was easy. I needed to get away from everybody; I badly needed space to do what needed to be done to sort the mess we were in. I needed to stay away until I got the opportunity to pay our bills and get back on track so that I could hold my head up high again. I also thought that if Seán was away from the people he drank with, that maybe things would be different. He was in full agreement. He would stay in Ireland with the kids while I made preparations for the family to move to London.

From September to December, I worked two jobs. I was in Superdrug during the day and doing bar work in the evenings with Wetherspoons. I would ring home every night or they would ring me; at that stage our phone bill was so high, there was no point in worrying about it and I really needed to hear my husband and children's voices every day. While I missed my family terribly, I also had a huge sense of joy at the possibility of having a new start. Although I knew the bills were still there, the fact that I was physically away from them meant that I felt free to come up with solutions to pay them. I was making decisions and availing of the opportunities that were around me and it felt good. I could sense that we were about to start anew.

MY PRIORITIES at the time were to save money, find schools for the children and a house for us to live in. Because of the circumstances of my upbringing, I had never had the chance to get to know my siblings properly but now there was an opportunity to finally spend time with Miriam and get to know her properly. It made sense, then, to stay in the Barnet area where I worked and where our families would be near each other, so I started scouting around the locality whenever I had a free minute.

One day while I was working in Superdrug, I learned a great lesson about the dangers of uninformed judgements and about how opportunity sometimes walks right up to you, there for the taking. The store manager had told the staff to keep an eye out for anyone who we thought was acting suspiciously. There was a bell under the counter we could ring to alert management and security if we thought someone was shoplifting. One morning, when I was at the tills and the shop was relatively quiet, a woman came in. She was middle aged and neatly dressed. She picked up a basket and spent a long time wandering between aisles, picking stuff up and putting it back on the shelves. I was wondering what she was doing and became suspicious. I pressed the bell and the manager appeared. I pointed to the woman and said she had been there for quite a while and that I thought she might be stealing. I had followed protocol and my job was done.

Eventually, the woman came to my till with her basket of items. We made small talk about the new store and she remarked on my Irish accent and asked what part of Ireland I was from. 'Kerry,' I said and she replied that she was originally from Cork. She was very friendly and I was soon telling her about myself. I said that I was new to London but was planning on bringing my family over as soon as I could get schools sorted for them, remarking that I wanted them to go to Catholic schools. She said she could help me, explaining that she was a religious Sister and the principal of St Martha's Senior School for girls at Hadley Wood. I nearly died of embarrassment; here was this woman offering to help me and I had thought— without any real foundation—that she was a shoplifter!

We arranged to meet a few days later at a nearby café during my lunch break. I still felt very bad about having thought she was shoplifting and realised that it is easy to be very wrong in our assumptions about people. When we met up again, the Sister said that St Martha's would suit my daughter but I interrupted her, saying there was no way we could afford to pay the fees at a private school. She said not to worry, she would sort that out.

For the older boys she recommended Finchley Catholic High School, which was near Barnet and which wasn't fee paying. The two smaller boys could go to St Catherine's where Miriam's children were pupils. The Sister said she would make all the calls and sort everything for me. All three schools were in a cluster around Barnet so it felt as if luck was definitely on my side. I was stunned and delighted. It was a huge burden lifted off my shoulders to have the children's schooling arranged as it was a very different system to the one in Ireland and more difficult for me to get my head around. Once the schools were sorted, our move was sealed.

The next big job was to find a new home for the entire family. Local free-sheets with rental listings were dropped into houses in the area every week so I consulted them. I was looking for a house not too far from Miriam's and soon found a two-storey property that would be available from December. It had three bedrooms upstairs and one downstairs, along with a kitchen-cum-dining room and a small sitting room. It wasn't very big and was very old-fashioned but it was a start and the rent was reasonable. I had a deposit saved so I paid that. Once the house was secured, I had a sense of hope after so many months of despair.

Seán packed up at home for the move. The kids seemed okay about leaving friends behind because they knew their cousins in London and were looking forward to meeting them. There was one child, however, who didn't want to leave home and who was unhappy with the move. The two eldest had warned against bringing the younger ones to England; they felt it was a bad idea to uproot them from their school and friends. But they didn't realise the extent of our debts or of the shame and pain I was going through which made it impossible for me to stay in Kerry.

It was vitally important for Seán and me to pay back what we owed. I had always been the partner who looked after the paying and managing of the bills and I just couldn't find headspace to see how that could be done in Kerry. I had to find work somewhere so it was either a city in Ireland or in England if we were to clean our financial slate. London was the better option; the recession had hit all of Ireland and I had family in London who would be a support to us. It was difficult to explain to the children why such an apparently radical move was so important, vital even. I always regretted, however, that I didn't make more of an effort to explain more clearly the reasons why we had to move.

OUR TWO eldest sons were already living and working in London and, in November, Seán made the journey to England by bus with the three youngest. I went to the station to meet them. I couldn't wait to hug them again; it was nearly ten weeks since I'd seen them and they had grown so much in that time. I noticed that one of them had a homemade haircut and was sporting a big gap in his fringe but that didn't matter. It was such a joy to be together again. The final two stayed in Ireland for a few more weeks to finish the secondary school term and they travelled over by bus in December.

We stayed with Miriam for a short time until our new home was available. It was pretty cramped at my sister's with so many of us living there and I knew we were really pushing the limits of her generosity and patience. Finally, our new home at Elton Avenue was ready and we moved in four days before Christmas 1990. It was great to have the whole family together again. The kids were fascinated with the adventure of it all and were happy to be under the one roof with both parents again.

That Christmas was absolutely brilliant; there was about three feet of snow on the ground and the younger children were delirious with joy—they had never seen so much snow in their lives. On Christmas Day we called to Miriam's and then we all went to Mass together. Seán cooked the dinner while the children played with their presents in between running in and out to play in the snow.

It was a very happy day for me and I felt I could relax after the whirlwind of the last few months. I had been totally focused on getting things ready for the family to come over—sorting the house and schools and saving money. I had worked as many hours as possible because I wanted to make sure there was money to buy presents that year as the previous Christmas had been very tough. All the family was together, we had food and gifts, there was snow on the ground; things weren't perfect but they were good and we were set for a new start in 1991.

THERE IS something about a fresh start that gives you renewed energy and I was full of passion and enthusiasm for our new life in London as the bells rang in the New Year. Seán and I talked and came up with a plan. We would work hard, harder than we had ever worked before, to create a good life for our family and to pay off our bills in Ireland. We knew it would take a few years, but we were very determined. Seán had found work playing music as soon as he had arrived the previous November. Live Irish music was very popular at the time and he played with our son Liam, mainly in Kilburn. A Killorglin man, Christy Kissane, had about five pubs in the area and he ensured they got several gigs a week.

We sorted out the school run; the boys were able to catch a bus to school and I would drop Mairead to St Martha's.

Her school was very posh, with huge rooms and polished floors. There was a big avenue up to it and it was quite intimidating to drive up to the main door. Students were dropped to school in black cabs if their parents weren't dropping them off in their top-of-the-range cars. We had invested in a van as soon as we could afford to buy a vehicle—a white Honda Acti—and I would drive Mairead to school in this. She had me warned to drop her off sufficiently distant from the entrance so that she wouldn't be spotted getting out of the van.

I understood her embarrassment. The wealth of the families attending the school was daunting and it was tough on her that we were different, though there were some funny moments, even if it was only in hindsight that we could laugh at them. I'll never forget her first day at the school; I had gotten the uniform from the school but they had no shoes in her size. I didn't have enough money to buy proper school shoes and instead gave her a pair of my own shoes for her first day. Unfortunately they were black stilettos. Mairead never forgot the sound of the heels clicking on the polished floors as she made her way to class.

There was another funny-after-the fact incident that happened when I was attending my first parent-teacher meeting. I decided to dress for the part and went to the local second-hand shops in Barnet where I normally shopped to look for something suitable. I was delighted when I found a very nice fur jacket. On the day of the meeting, I parked well away from the building and made my way up the avenue. I was hoping to meet the Sister who had facilitated Mairead's entrance to the school but there was no sign of her. I sat with a group of mothers who were also waiting to meet the teachers and made small talk with them.

Mairead spotted me and came over; within a few minutes a look of horror came over her face. 'What's the matter?' I asked. 'Did you see what's hanging off the back of your jacket?' she said. I hadn't but it was a Barnardos tag with '£5' written on it. I told her to tear it off which she did before taking off down the hall as quickly as she could. I was more concerned about upsetting her than of embarrassing myself. I could see there was a lot of 'keeping up with the Joneses' going on in the school and that it was going to be a hard road for Mairead, yet she made some very close friends there which was a great relief.

There was one day that gave me a laugh. I drove to the school to collect Mairead on what was one of the worst days ever. The rain was torrential so I drove right up to the entrance where she and a few friends were trying to shelter from the downpour, breaking the golden rule that I would not drive the van up the avenue. I told them all to hop in. The girls got into the back of the van where I had a mattress for the younger kids for ferrying them around. Mairead had a face like thunder and I got a fit of laughing and started singing because it was all so hilarious. My daughter, however, didn't see the funny side of the situation until much later; that event is now a cherished family memory that we all laugh about.

The boys got on well in St Catherine's and Finchley Catholic High School. They made good friends who loved coming back to our house because of all the fun and chaos that was there. Homework had to be done as soon as the kids came home from school and Seán was great at helping them with it. We were both anxious that they did well at school. Because neither Seán nor I had gone through the full education cycle, third level education wasn't high on the agenda, particularly given the number of kids we had and considering how much college would cost. That said, several of them did go on to further education, with two eventually attending college in London and most of the others going to college in Ireland.

WHILE I was working in Superdrug, I was always looking out for something better. Slattery's, whose buses I had cleaned in Kerry, had a travel agency in Kentish Town and I made initial contact with them before the family came over to see if they would have anything suitable for me. I had experience working in a travel agency since my years at McSweeney's; in fact, my varied work there was a fantastic foundation for my future work life.

By the end of 1990, I had a job lined up at Slattery's in the office. I had never used a computer before but was assured that everything would be fine and that I would pick it up easily enough. I would be getting £100 a week which was about the same as my average wages from Superdrug, but I had no set hours there and had to wait from week to week to know what the roster would be. With so many children it was difficult to juggle everything so I thought if I had a job that was nine to six, Monday to Friday, it would be better. I could also do extra work if I needed to.

I started work in the travel agency in January 1991 but while I was trying to come to grips with using their computer system, I was also very preoccupied. Since leaving Kerry, I had wanted to make contact with the banks back home, to let them know that we were now living in London and working to try and pay off our debts. I kept putting it off until one day, in February 1991, I went out at lunch time and bought envelopes and a notepad. I was very nervous but I knew this had to be done; I had to take the first steps in tackling the issue of our debts.

The first letter I wrote was to the mortgage company in Dublin. At that stage I didn't know if we, in fact, still owned the house because I hadn't opened their letters in the previous few years and didn't know what was in them. I apologised for not answering their correspondence and explained that we had left the house and that my mother had a set of keys if they wanted them. I wrote that the family was in London and that both Seán and I were working. I added that I understood why they might take the house off us but that, if they would bear with us and give us the opportunity, we would pay back the arrears plus the mortgage. With a mixture of fear and relief, I put the letter in an envelope and posted it. That was the first of many such letters.

About two weeks later, a letter appeared in the post box from the mortgage company. I was afraid to open it, as had been my habitual reaction for several years, but I eventually forced myself to do what I most feared. The response of the mortgage company amazed me. They said they were sorry to hear about our circumstances and, as I had written to them and been honest about our situation, they would accept our offer of £5 a week to pay off the arrears in addition to paying the mortgage in full, which was about £200 per month. They said they would not repossess the house as long as we didn't miss a payment.

In disbelief, I asked Seán to read the letter again, saying, 'Am I after reading it right?'. When I realised that we wouldn't lose the house, I was so happy that I actually jumped with joy on the bed. If we had lost our home, returning to Ireland would have been so much more difficult. Getting that letter from the mortgage company brought light and hope into our lives. I now knew that we could deal with the other bills and creditors—the electricity bill, the phone bill, the small suppliers and the credit union. I wrote back immediately and thanked them and said that, by the end of the month, they would have the money.

From then on I posted the money directly to them every month; there were no direct transfers and no online banking then. One time, however, I posted the money and they didn't get it. They contacted me to say we had missed a payment. I knew the money had been stolen but there was nothing I could do about it. I was in a terrible state and rang my mother to tell her that the house payment had gone missing and we didn't have any other money to replace it.

We had rented the house in Kerry at this stage and my mother would collect the rent and pay bits off our other local bills. Now she had to collect this money, and any other few pounds she could get her hands on, so I could pay the mortgage. There was no way we could risk losing the house. From then on, I went to the post office and sent the money by postal order and we never again had a problem with the mortgage company. That was the biggest weight off my mind. At least now we would have a home to return to when the time came.

I SPENT about seven months at the travel agency in Kentish Town and hated every minute of it. I just couldn't get a handle on how to use the computer no matter how hard I tried. I wanted to learn but I couldn't and became very frustrated; I couldn't even manage the basics. Then the office manager said she would change me to accounts. I said I had never done accounts before but I would have a try; it was a disaster. I think that I wasn't able to master the skills because I had so much in my head at the time—I'd had to organise the house, the schools, the kids coming over, I was working and I went into this new job with the expectation that it would be easy and then there was this computerised system that I couldn't master or even focus on.

While the office manager was very nice at the start, as the months passed she grew impatient with me. I decided after about five months that I had to leave. One evening, when I was on the way home, I saw a sign on a health clinic window near to where we lived. It said, 'Cleaner wanted, evenings 6-8pm'. I took down the number and rang them. We set up a meeting and they offered me the work. I explained that I was working nine to six but if they would allow me time to get from the travel agency to the clinic, I could start at 6.15pm. To my amazement, they agreed and each day, as soon as I was finished in Kentish Town, I quickly made the fifteen-minute journey back to Barnet and did my two-hour shift. I earned £50 a week there and liked the work so much that I looked forward to leaving the office and heading to the clinic.

Even though the cleaning was adding two hours to my working day (not counting what had to be done when I got home), I still enjoyed it a lot more than the work at the travel agency. Naturally, it was unsustainable and after a couple of months I knew that I couldn't keep both jobs. I had a decision to make: I knew I really liked the cleaning work and that the job in Kentish Town was breaking my spirit. I also knew that the people at the clinic were happy with my work so I asked if they had work at any other clinics. They had and were glad to give it to me. I gave in my notice at the travel agency and starting cleaning both clinics.

I was earning the same money as I had been at the travel agency and I had also regained my headspace. I hated being tied in an office where I couldn't move around. This proved to me that if you are in a job you don't like, you won't be happy no matter what you are earning. There might not be many people who prefer a cleaning job to working in a travel agency, but I did. I believe you should always go with what you like—it doesn't matter what it is—because you will be good at it.

My daily schedule saw me clean one of the clinics in the morning before it opened and the other in the evening after it closed. I was given the keys to both clinics and I would lock up when I was done. The older children came to the clinic with me in the evening as it was only a few minutes from our house. They would empty the bins and do a bit of vacuuming and we would often be out of there by half past seven.

I wanted more work but, as I was already doing mornings and evenings, I knew I would have to get different and more flexible cleaning hours. I looked up the local paper and saw that there was a cleaning job going in the police station close to the clinic where I was already working. I rang and left my details but didn't hear anything back. In the meantime, I put up some 'Cleaner available' notices and started picking up bits and pieces of private house cleaning. Then, six weeks after I had applied for the job in the police station, I got a letter from them saying that they had done a background check on me and that I had been cleared. There was a lot of unrest in London at the time due to the Troubles in Northern Ireland and Irish people were coming under increased security screening. Nonetheless, I got the job which had to be done between five and seven in the morning.

Seán and I were now working together again, earning about £5 each an hour. There were three sections to the police station and we had the bottom section where the cells were. When the middle floor cleaner left, they asked us to take it on; then the top floor became available and we took that on too. The pair of us did the three floors together, with Seán starting a bit earlier than me. Then we were asked if we could take on another police station in Whetstone, near to where the second health clinic was. To accommodate us, they allowed us do one station at night and the other in the morning. Our work situation was improving by the week.

CHAPTER FIVE

LEARNING
LIFE'S LESSONS

A T THE END of 1991, we moved house to Horsham Avenue as the owner of the house in Elton Avenue was moving back into her property. Life was busy but good then. Seán and two of our boys played music very regularly and I would go out once a week with Miriam to a bar around the corner from our new home and we would have a drink and play darts or pool. I loved pool and got a name for being quite good at it. I found our neighbours and the locals friendly enough but I didn't make any close friends. I got on well with the people I was working for and, after that, I didn't really have time to develop close personal relationships.

I went home twice a year; always in January for my mother's birthday, with one or two of the younger children, and for two weeks in August when the whole family would go back to Kerry on Slattery's bus. We stayed in our own house and my sister Joan would give us the loan of her car to drive into Tralee to see my parents. My mother didn't ever travel to London to visit us although Seán's mother and family came over regularly.

Over the next year, word of mouth spread about our cleaning business and people wanted to know how to contact us. We needed a name and a phone number and came up with the name 'Mitchels Cleaning Service' because Seán was from the Mitchels area in Tralee. People assumed that Mitchel was our name and would say 'Hello Mr and Mrs Mitchel', which had us in fits of laughter. We had a lot of work coming in, much more than two of us could manage on our own. Our older sons were great at helping out and my sisters Miriam and Áine, who also lived in London, worked with us as well. In fact, depending on the work to be done, there could have been up to ten of us working at a given time. We kept our overheads low; we had a van and a vacuum cleaner for the private houses, as well as some basic cleaning products. The health clinics had their own equipment and cleaning agents as the work there was very specialised. We also cleaned some bars which was handy work as we could do it in the late morning.

Word of mouth continued to work very well for our cleaning services and, by 1992, we had so much work that we couldn't take on any more contracts. We did individual houses, though not too many. I clearly remember one house in the upmarket Totteridge area that we cleaned a few times. It was absolutely enormous and the sitting room had a white carpet and white leather couches. I had to take my shoes off at the door and the owner would have a pair of slippers ready for me to put on.

She was very fussy and would check every single thing that I did. I was warned that the vacuum cleaner was not to leave a scratch on her beautiful high skirting boards. I learned a lot of skills from my time there, in terms of the care that is needed when you are in someone's home. However, despite the fact that the owners were immensely wealthy, they were only paying £4 an hour (less than what we were earning elsewhere). I asked her for more money as it wasn't worth my while doing the job for the rate she was paying but she wouldn't budge so I didn't continue there.

GENERALLY, I would be up at five, gone for half past five and back again by about ten o'clock in the morning. I would do the housework, prepare the dinner and try to get an hour's sleep before the kids came home from school. I was almost always there in the evening when they came in and then I went out again and worked from five until ten at night. All my life, I've never slept more than four hours; five hours would be a long night's sleep for me. When I came home at night I would get lunches and other stuff ready for the next day. We worked weekends as well, on Saturday and Sunday mornings, though I didn't work on those evenings. Nonetheless, I was out of the house an awful lot, as was Seán, who played music at night and worked with me in the mornings.

The kids always helped out with the cleaning work, and when both Seán and I were both out working, the older ones looked after the younger ones. I remember them commenting sometimes that I wasn't at home to give them their breakfast. They would have to get up and get themselves ready and I would leave money for their bus fares. They weren't going hungry, far from it, but now I wasn't there in the home when they wanted me. I knew I wasn't seeing enough of them, or having enough time with them doing things other than work. It is one of my biggest regrets that I worked all those hours and that I wasn't there when I should have been. I know that this skewed work-life balance affected the kids.

One of the children never really settled in London; he hadn't wanted to come over and he wasn't a bit content. He returned to Ireland at one stage and stayed with family, though he later rejoined us in London. Our daughter wasn't that keen either but she wasn't as unsettled as her brother. My attitude was that we had to make the best of it but our son continued to be unhappy throughout our time in the city. I probably didn't deal with his unhappiness in the way I should have done; work and earning enough money to pay off what we owed was what this period in our lives was all about for me. We always intended returning to Ireland, but not until we had enough money to pay those bills and have a clean start back home.

My motivation to pay our debts was huge and I was trying to save as well. No matter what our outgoings were— and there were a lot of them with such a big family—I was always trying to save some bit. If it was only £5 a week, I would put it away and it would build up. I learned a lot about money management during these years. Before that, we had spent money as quickly as it was made. Within a space of two years in London, we had built up our cleaning work to the point where there was a combined substantial amount coming into the house on a weekly basis. Our older sons continued to play music and they would also contribute to the running of the household. We weren't a materialistic family; we just bought what we needed; in fact, all we ever owned was a van. This meant that we could afford to live a basic but decent life as well as pay off our debts.

WE WERE making good headway paying off our debts and I remember talking to Seán one night and saying that things were finally turning around for us. The kids were growing up (the youngest was almost six), our mortgage was finally under control, and we were also making a bit of money. We were still working very hard and while I had always been well able for the work, I found as the spring of 1992 progressed that I had less energy and was getting tired more easily. It entered my head that I might have cancer. I went to the doctor and discovered that I was pregnant; I couldn't believe it. I went home and told Seán, who was equally shocked.

There was so much to think about: I was forty-two and worried if the baby would be okay at my age. What would it be like to give birth in a city where I knew nothing about their maternity system? Would I be able to continue working? But side by side with my concerns was the thought that it would be lovely to have another girl, a sister for Mairead. After Seán and I talked it through some more, my worries lessened and all I wanted was that our baby would be born healthy and that we would look after her or him as best we could.

I was embarrassed telling our older children that I was pregnant but all went well and I was soon flying again. I always blossomed when I was pregnant and I didn't miss a day at work. Seán's mother and aunt came over in May for the confirmation of one of the children. We hadn't told anybody in Ireland that I was expecting but now the secret was out. When I told them the news, Seán's mother said, 'Are you joking? Were you not going to tell anyone and just arrive in Ireland with a baby?'. 'That's exactly what would have happened,' I answered. Then I had to ring home and tell them all. I hadn't planned to break the news until after the birth because I didn't want them to worry, what with me now being an older mother. In spite of my worries, the pregnancy proceeded very well.

The baby was due on the 14th of August but, as none of our children had arrived on their due date, Seán went to work as normal that morning. Our routine was that he would take the first bus and leave me the van to take the kids to school and then I would follow him to work. I felt fine before he left but, when I got up, I got a pain that nearly floored me. I called one of the boys and said I needed him to ring for an ambulance. When it arrived, I told him not to tell the younger ones that I was gone to hospital but to let on I was gone to work because I didn't want them getting all excited and upset. I asked him to stay at home as I would need to ring the house with my news and he would have to convey the information to Seán. These were the days before mobile phones.

When I got into the hospital, I asked the nurse if she could do a quick examination. I told her that I thought it was a false alarm, adding that I needed to get back to work. She looked at me and said, 'You're going nowhere. Your baby will be born soon'. I rang home to let my son know the news and to ask him to tell his father to come into the hospital as soon as possible. Seán had to do a double shift to cover my work and didn't arrive until half eleven. This would be my eighth time giving birth and he'd never been present for any of the births. I hadn't wanted him in the delivery room and it wasn't the done thing at the time in Ireland. This time, however, I was very nervous and when I saw him I told him he had to stay beside me until the baby arrived.

The nurse offered me an epidural and I said no; I'd never had one before and didn't want one now. Then, as the pain became unbearable, I changed my mind. 'Too late,' she said, 'your baby will be born shortly.' That was twenty-five past twelve and at five past one our second daughter, Ciara, was born. I looked at her in my arms and felt a surge of pure love. I was delighted to have a second girl; finally a sister for Mairead after all the brothers. Seán headed home to tell the children the news. Mairead, who was fifteen at the time, said, 'It's a bit too late to get a sister, she is no use to me'. However, it wasn't long before they became the best of friends.

I wanted to have a shower but the nurse said I would have to wait a while. 'You might think you are fine but you are not,' she warned. After a while I grew sick of waiting and got out of the bed to go for my shower. I took a bit of a stagger. The nurse returned and I was put promptly back into bed.

That time, they would leave you out after a couple of hours, especially if you had given birth before. If the baby was born before twelve noon you could go home the same day. The doctor came in and examined the baby and all was perfect; then he examined me. 'We normally let mothers out on the same day but you have a big family at home and need rest so I want you to stay overnight,' he said. I really wanted to get out of there and told him that my children were almost fully grown and that I would have lots of rest at home as I had plenty of people to care for me and the new baby.

Seán phoned me at three and I asked him to come in to collect me. 'Are you joking?' he said, in disbelief, 'I was talking to the doctor and he said you are not being left out for two days.' Then I rang Miriam and told her I was going home at six o'clock and needed her to come for me in a taxi, which she did. I arrived home with the baby in my arms. Seán was horrified but the children were so charmed by their new sister that he forgot to give out to me for leaving the hospital early. He had a pre-booked gig somewhere and Miriam said she would stay with me while he and Liam were out. I said I wanted to go to the gig and asked Miriam to stay and mind the kids. 'Are you for real?' Seán asked. Miriam threatened to go home if I went out. I think I was slightly delirious and, in the end, I stayed put.

At the end of the week, I started to haemorrhage badly and was rushed to hospital by ambulance. I thought I was going to die. I realised then that I had come out too soon and had gone back to work too early, only a week after the birth. I was kept in for almost two weeks and Ciara was with me during that time. I made a full recovery although the experience had shaken me and I didn't go back to work for about two weeks after that. For the next while, Seán and I did our shifts separately so there was always one of us at home. He would get the older boys to give a hand doing the clinics in the mornings. After a few weeks, we went back to our usual routine. Mairead minded Ciara and would ring me if the baby woke up as I was just a few minutes away at the police station. She was like a little mommy and all the others were great with their new sister as well.

LIFE was exceptionally busy with the new baby and at work but I wanted my family in Kerry to meet Ciara so I went home for a flying visit in November 1992. A few of the younger children came with me. We travelled by bus as usual and when we got to Kerry I met up with everybody. I got a bit of a shock when I saw my sister Joan. I knew she had been ill but she was a very private person and wasn't inclined to open up about what was wrong with her. It was coming up to Christmas and she would usually be full of the joys of getting ready for the festivities but this year she seemed very down. She was complaining of pains in her side, her back and her stomach. I could see her taking sharp intakes of breath and advised her to go to the doctor. Then we got caught up in the excitement of the new baby and I was back in London before I knew it.

A few weeks later, on the 22nd of December, we were all at home on a Sunday night, sitting in front of the fire, watching some programme on TV. I heard a knock, as did my son who was sitting nearest to me. Nobody else heard it but my son went to the door and I followed him out. There wasn't anybody there and I got a dreadful sense of foreboding. I had just said to Seán that this wasn't a good sign when the phone rang. I was so relieved to hear Joan's voice. She told me that our father had taken a turn and was very bad. I said I would ring back later to see how he was. In fact, I rang back almost immediately and said, 'He's gone, isn't he?'. She said that he was. He had been dancing in the local community centre that afternoon when he got a heart attack.

I was in shock; my father hadn't been ill and at seventy-one he wasn't very old. I rang my siblings who were living in England at the time and we discussed what we would do. We were waiting to hear further about arrangements and to find out how the funeral would be planned over the Christmas holiday but then we decided that we would just go ahead and book flights as we needed to get home to our mother, irrespective of what days the funeral would be on.

We flew back to Ireland together. At the main terminal in the airport there was a bomb alert. I kept shouting, 'Avoid the bins! Avoid the bins!', as it was common that terrorists would put bombs in dustbins. We were running and when I looked back I could see one of my sisters lagging far behind us; she wasn't too quick on her feet and, probably out of nervousness, I got a fit of laughing and then we were all laughing even though we were genuinely scared that there was a bomb about to go off. 'We'll have no luck for this!' Miriam said.

When we arrived in Kerry we were told that the burial would take place on the 26th as no burials were conducted on Christmas Day. We went to the funeral home to view the body and then went back to my parents' house in Hawley Park. My mother was not in a good way. She didn't want anyone coming into the house because she didn't think it looked good enough. Then she said she wasn't feeling well herself so she went to the doctor. The upshot was that she was sent to hospital and missed the funeral. She suffered from regular attacks of emphysema but I think she just couldn't deal with having to meet people and going to hospital was her opt-out.

All of my siblings attended the funeral. My father had not been the best of fathers by any stretch and he had failed all of us in so many ways throughout the years. Somehow, in spite of all that, I'd managed to have a reasonable relationship with him. When I'd ring home, we would chat on the phone and he would love to see us visiting, especially when we gave him a few pounds. He didn't ask for it when we were adults but he was always glad to take the money. He was never a proper provider; even when they grew old, my mother couldn't wait to qualify for the old-age pension so that she would have her own money. He did mellow as the years passed and he was good to my mother after they moved into Tralee and when she suffered from depression. He'd prepare her food and take it to her room on the days when she didn't get up, and there were many of those. By the time he died, my overwhelming feeling for him was one of pity; I felt sorry for the very flawed human being that he had been.

BY 1993, the family was growing up and we needed more space. The house we were living in was becoming cramped with ten of us in it and I was on the lookout for a more suitable property. I've always been good at making people out and, through informal networking, I came across a woman who worked for a community organisation that sourced larger houses for bigger families. She soon found a house for us in Whetstone. The rent was lower than it had been in our previous home and the house was bigger, so it was a win-win situation for us.

However, even though we had a new and more spacious home, we were thinking that it mightn't be more than another few years before we would be able to return to Ireland with a good foundation from which to start anew. We had good, dependable contracts and were working hard but, after the death of my father, I started thinking more about my mother being alone and was more focused than ever on getting our final debts paid off so that we could return home.

The kids had never lost contact with their cousins and friends in Ireland and I knew that they would be happy to return too. Every time we went home on holiday, they loved it. I had kept in regular contact with all the family in Ireland and with people I was friendly with, and really enjoyed catching up with them by phone and when we were home on our annual two-week holiday. I was coming to recognise that I was lonely in London; I hadn't made any new friends there. I did have my sister close by and she was a great support but I missed my friends in Kerry. That, plus the fact that my mother was alone and getting older, and the knowledge that Joan was sick, made me think more and more about when we might be able to return.

I wasn't feeling great in the August of 1993 when we went home for our annual holiday; my health wasn't good and work was getting on top of me. One lovely sunny afternoon before we returned to London, I was chatting to Joan and telling her what was going on in my mind. She turned to me and said, 'Breeda, why don't you come home? What are you doing over there if you want to be back home?'. I also spoke with Rita West, a very good friend of mine, and told her that I really wanted to come home. 'Why don't you?' she said. 'You could do what you are doing in London here.' The economy had picked up by then and there were several new businesses opening around the county. She said there was a niche in the market for contract cleaners in Kerry and in the wider Munster region.

The thought hadn't registered with me until she said it. Sometimes we don't see the most obvious things but once it was pointed out to me, the seeds for our return home were planted there and then. We were now well ahead with our debt repayments and we had never intended staying longer than five years in London anyhow. I started planning: there was no central heating in the house in Farmers' Bridge so I began saving specifically to have a heating system installed.

FOR MANY YEARS, long before we went to London, Joan was complaining of pains in her stomach. That said, she was always full of energy and compassion, forever running around looking after others. She was a mom to all of us and was a great homemaker. She was one of those people who loved without question and who was loved in return. She was also a very private person and, while I knew that her pains were increasing, when I would ask her how she was, she would say she was not too bad or that she was fine. I advised her to go to the doctor but that was about the extent of the conversation she would allow about her health. She had always been slight but, in August 1993, I was shocked by how thin she had become. We all realised then that there was something serious wrong with her. We suspected that she had cancer but the 'C' word was out of bounds and not to be mentioned in her presence.

During that summer, she spent a lot of time by the sea in Castlegregory at her mobile home. She loved being there, reading and taking in the healthy sea air. By autumn, however, her health started to deteriorate more rapidly. Her sister-in-law was a close friend and confidante and she was also a nurse. She was the one that Joan finally confided in that she did, in fact, have cancer. She had been given a diagnosis in Ireland and had then come to London for a second opinion. That opinion confirmed the original diagnosis. It was only then that she let us know officially that she had the dreaded disease, but she still didn't want to talk about it. She got her treatment and lived her life, with good days and bad days. When I rang her or she rang me, I would ask her how she was but I would never mention the word cancer; she hated it.

By early 1994, however, we knew she wasn't going to make it. I came home in January for our mother's birthday and Joan was very sick at this time. After I returned to London, I would ring and if she didn't answer the phone, I would know she wasn't well. If she answered, she would be in good form. If she was feeling in any way okay, she would be back to her usual energetic self. Around Easter that year, I phoned her and she was after tearing the house asunder to clean it; she was a dinger at the cleaning and loved it. She told me she was off to take a bath—a treat she loved—after cleaning the house from top to bottom.

However, within weeks, in early June, I got a call from her husband Pádraig to say we needed to come home, that Joan was very ill and wanted to see all her siblings. Miriam, Áine and I travelled together from London. We stayed with my mother in Tralee and she warned us that Joan was very weak and that we should be prepared. We went out to her beautiful home in Ballyseedy. We waited for a long time in the kitchen because Joan wanted to look her best for us and her sister-in-law was helping her to put on make-up and her wig.

When she was ready, we went into her bedroom, one at a time. After I entered, she asked me to get into the bed beside her. I did and she put her arms around me. 'I am dying but I am at peace,' she said. 'I am happy and have accepted my fate. The reason I wanted to see you is to tell you to make sure you look after yourself first and then your children. Come home and you will be fine.' She told me how good I was and that she loved me. Then she said goodbye. I left the room. She did this with each one of us there that day. When we looked into her room sometime later, she was asleep. Between this final visit and when she died she couldn't talk on the phone so that day was the last time I spoke to her.

A few days later, on the 17th of June, I got a call to say that my beautiful, funny, loving sister had died. She was forty years old. I wasn't able to come home for the funeral, a fact that devastated me. While I had been on that final visit home to see Joan, our older daughter had become ill with quinsy, a potentially serious complication of tonsillitis, and I had been forced to return to London earlier than expected. Mairead had to go to hospital and she was so ill I was terrified that she, too, was going to die. When I got the news that Joan had passed away, I felt that I just couldn't leave the younger children again and go back to Ireland.

LATER that year, in August, when we all came home for our annual family holiday, I was feeling very unwell. I had a bad flu that I couldn't shake; in fact, I'd had to cancel some work because of it. I was suffering from stress and was feeling that I couldn't continue living as I was any longer. I had this overwhelming emotional need to come home. I was anxious to meet my mother and the other family members to talk about Joan, and to meet with her husband and children.

That year's holiday home was sad. We stayed in our house in Farmers' Bridge but I spent a lot of time with my mother in Tralee. My flu didn't go away while we were in Kerry and on our return journey, by plane from Farranfore, the flight was delayed and I was hit by a panic attack. I thought we were all going to die if we got on the plane. When the time came to board, I was in a bad state. The situation was exacerbated by the fact that Seán started drinking while we were waiting at the airport. He had struggled with the disease of alcoholism over the years and had been in a good place for much of the time. However, in recent months he had been drinking more often. That, added to all the other things that had happened—Joan's death, my own failing health and the thought of my mother living alone—meant that I was on a downward emotional spiral.

We arrived safely in London and the next day I went back to work but, by the end of the week, I was so sick I could barely stand. I went to the doctor and was told that I had double pneumonia and pleurisy. The fact that I'd had TB made me more susceptible to such illnesses and I was always in dread of getting as much as a chest cold because of that weakness in my body. The doctor said that I would be dead in six months if I didn't take a break. I was so ill, the sickest I had ever been, so I came home and went straight to bed.

The doctor had said to give the medication three or four days to work and, if I didn't improve in that time, I would definitely have to go to hospital. That frightened me so I stayed indoors because I wanted to get better. I continued to improve and on Sunday evening I was hit, as if by a bolt of lightning, by a thought: it was time to go home to Ireland. To this day, I don't know how it came to me so clearly and definitively, although I do think that my deteriorating health was the determining factor. 'I'll be home today week,' I said to Seán. At that point in time, I didn't care if he came with me or not. I knew the younger kids were ready to go back home and I also knew that I was at the end of my tether.

It felt familiar in a way; in 1990—what seemed like a lifetime ago—I knew that we had to go to England to start a new life and get our finances sorted; now it was imperative to return home. Two family members had died and I knew I hadn't dealt with their passing and couldn't if I continued with the breakneck life we were living in London. The time for another new beginning had arrived.

The next morning I rang the schools the kids had been attending in Kerry before we left and asked if they would accept them for the new school year. They were thrilled to be getting additional pupils. I went to the police stations and the clinics and told them that I was going home. I explained that I had been to the doctor and had been advised to work less; the children were young, I said, and I wanted to be around for them and to see them growing up. Seán said he would stay on and continue with the cleaning contracts. I said that was fine. It was the first time in my life I didn't care whether or not the work was done; I was going home to Ireland and that was it.

I rang my mother and she was delighted. I was overjoyed that she had something to be happy about for the first time in a long while. The kids were thrilled when they heard the news. The four youngest would be coming home with me and the three oldest would stay on in London; they were adults now and old enough to make their own decisions. Mairead, who was eighteen at the time, was already back home. When we had visited in August, she had applied for a job in Tralee. She had always planned on returning and when she got news that she'd been given the job, she made the journey back to Kerry.

THERE WAS a lot of packing to be done and we were lucky to have a Transit van. This had replaced a Honda van we had paid £300 for and which stalled one day before the engine blew up. The Transit had cost £1,000 and had great space in it. We managed to put in two beds and all the clothes, toys and bits and pieces that we could, including the pet hamster. I drove away from the house in Whetstone without any regret.

I felt nervous driving the kids through the London traffic and had several drivers beeping at me. Our oldest son said he would drive in front of me as I'd never driven outside the city before and we were travelling to Fishguard in Wales to take the ferry home. He pulled in at some point and I ran into the back of his car; I think it was caused by nerves from driving a van full of children, pets and household items to our new life. At customs, the officer opened the back of the van and the hamster fell out and we all roared laughing. I wasn't laughing as much, however, when I tried to drive off the ferry in the midst of the huge articulated lorries into whose lane we had been directed with our van.

Finally, we arrived back in Ireland. We sang all the way home, a journey of about five hours. We were tired but I had a real sense that we were heading in the right direction to a new and good beginning. I felt lightheaded coming across the County Bounds into Kerry; I looked at the sign and at the natural beauty around us and was delighted. The kids were shouting, 'Are we home yet? Are we home yet?'.

I'll never forget the feeling when I turned the corner outside our house and drove up the drive; it was brilliant. Mairead was at the door to meet us and the kids were delighted, absolutely thrilled: we were finally home. We emptied the van straightaway; there was no time for a rest, such was the excitement. The house still had furniture and all the stuff we hadn't taken to London was in the room where we had stored it. It was all hands on deck to unpack and then I drove into town to buy groceries. We had definitely earned our tea.

We had come home on a Sunday and the children were back in school on the Monday. They knew some of their classmates because we had kept close connections all along and they settled in very quickly. I, too, settled in immediately. I felt ready for this new life we were about to embark on: all our debts were paid off and we had around £5,000 in savings. It was September and the first job was to get the heating sorted and then we would be set. I was never as sure in my life that I had done the right thing.

BACK IN LONDON, Seán and the boys were sorting things out. They moved out of the large house and found more suitable accommodation while Seán continued with as much of the work as possible. Then, about a month or so after I had returned home, he decided to come home too. His most recent relapse into drinking had upset me a lot following my sister's death. I felt that he was throwing his life away whereas she had been given no choice. Joan's death was definitely a turning point for me; it was a wake-up call to examine what was going on in my own life.

I drove over to collect Seán and at the end of the journey home, when we stopped at our front door, I spoke openly to him. I said that he was a great husband and father but with my recent illnesses and the deaths in the family I just found I could no longer cope with the drinking bouts. I wasn't angry or bitter, I was just done. It was time for something to change. I could see that the disease was affecting everyone in the family. I knew that he had tried his best but I also knew that I could no longer cope with his illness and that I would prefer if he lived in town until he sorted himself out. Something clicked and this time he decided to find the help he needed. He tapped into the courage and compassion needed to help him give up drinking.

IT WAS very difficult for me when Seán first became sober because I was now dealing with a new person. Every day I could see him getting better and I wasn't quite sure how to deal with this new scenario but I returned to Al-Anon and got great support there. Once I remembered to focus on my own actions and reactions, it became a lot easier.

It was wonderful to have the man I had fallen in love with all those years ago back again. We were always a team on our shared journey through life and, with his health back, I knew we could achieve anything we set our minds to.

As soon as Seán felt sure of his health again, we set out on the next phase of our life together. This was a new adventure where we needed each other, working as a close team with a shared vision and goal. There was no one I would have wanted to start out with again other than my lovely husband. Through all of our years together, my love for him had remained as strong as it originally was and, to this day, I still love to see him coming in the door. The love and the bond are still there, as strong as ever.

CHAPTER SIX

STARTING OVER

I'M A FIRM BELIEVER in starting anew and being ready to begin again; in always learning and finding out how we can do things better. And, at the end of 1994, our family was about to begin again, back in the place where we had started but with so much more knowledge and experience under our belts. Seán and I, along with those of our children who were now adults, looked at the bigger picture to ascertain what we had and what we could do. As soon as we left London, our business there evaporated; all we retained from our time there were the experience and skills we had gained which were, in fact, priceless. We had some savings that would tide us over for a while and Seán could resume his music playing career, which he did, though to a lesser extent than previously.

Our plan was to set up a professional contract cleaning business in Kerry; we knew and liked this work and—vitally—we were very good at it. We wanted to do it right so we were happy to take it step by step, and not rush into anything based on the assumption that all would work out just because we had built up a body of experience in London. I went to Citizens Advice on an information-gathering exercise. I explained that I wanted to set up a business and asked what supports, if any, existed for someone in my position. They told me about the Back To Work allowance which I could avail of and which would allow me some breathing space while the various components were put in place to set up the new business. To qualify for this allowance, you had to sign on the dole for a specific period of time, which I did.

I did a Start Your Own Business course which was run by the Enterprise Board. I learned there about the many formalities of setting up and running a business, including how to do a business plan, how to sort out insurance, the importance of marketing and solid sales, and the many other aspects of running a business, some of which I had already been doing without necessarily knowing where they fit into an overall business plan. I had paid the mortgage for about four months in advance, so that outgoing was covered until January 1995 but we still needed cash coming into the house while we were in the planning stages for our business. I was, as ever, on the lookout for any work that I could pick up and spotted an opportunity during a regular outing with my younger children who loved going to the bowling alley in Tralee. I noticed that the restaurant was closed and asked my brother, who was working there, why that was the case. He said the owner, who was a businessman, didn't have anybody to run it.

I started thinking about how this might work as a money-earner for us. The venue was very popular at the time; it was large and could accommodate a lot of people and it was open seven days a week. I approached the owner and said that I would run the restaurant (which had a fully-equipped kitchen) if he gave it to me rent-free. I would pay my electricity bill and would clean the whole bowling alley for free. Another plus for the owner was that the restaurant would attract more people and give those already attending a reason to stay longer and maybe play more games of bowling. He agreed immediately.

Everything was covered under the one insurance, which the owner paid. All I had to do was get a supplier for the food and soft drinks. The kitchen was really nice and once I started working there, I did lunches as well as evening meals. I knew this wasn't going to be a long-term project but it worked well for the time we had it; we were able to feed ourselves and Seán and the older children were happy to pitch in when I needed additional help if a tournament or some other event was taking place. This business was great to tide us over for a period of time while the preparatory work was being done to set up our cleaning business.

Once I had completed the Start Your Own Business course, I was able to work full time and draw the Back To Work allowance simultaneously: it was time to start our business. One night, we all sat around the table at home, determined to come up with a name for the new business. It had to start with the letter A because A is the first letter in the alphabet and, so, would be at the top of any directory or listing. Someone suggested 'All Brite Cleaning Services'. That sounded perfect and I officially registered the name in April 1995. I gave up the bowling alley, got business cards printed and put my first ad in *Kerry's Eye* newspaper. We bought the basics that we needed for cleaning, including a ladder and a vacuum cleaner. We were ready for business with Seán and I working together as the core team.

Our first job came from Ned O'Shea, the businessman I had liaised with regarding the bowling alley. He was also a builder and, before I left the bowling alley, I had told him about our cleaning business and asked him to consider us for any work that he might have. By then, I had learned the important lesson that you have to ask for what you want; it is vitally important to let people know what you need and not be afraid to ask for it. Ned, in fact, gave us all his cleaning work. He was building new houses in west and north Kerry and we would do the initial cleans.

Our very first job with him was in Dingle and when we got it, Seán had to leave early in the morning to drive there because the only way we had of transporting the ladder was by having it sticking in through one window and out through the other with a red rag hanging off it. It wasn't the best or safest way to travel and he set off as early as possible so that the chances of meeting another vehicle were minimised. Our Transit van had fallen apart soon after we returned to Kerry and we had bought a car because we couldn't afford to get a replacement van. As soon as we started cleaning again, we knew that using the car wasn't suitable for work, so, in the summer of 1995, we bought 'Betsy', a small red van that cost about £700.

Mobile phones were becoming more common and I decided it was time for me to get one. My birthday is in May and the family clubbed together to buy a phone as my present. I was delighted with my first phone which went on to become a source of great amusement. It was absolutely huge and weighed as much as a heavy brick but I didn't care; I had a mobile number now and was sure the calls would come flooding in. I had just got it when I went to visit my mother. I was boasting to her and some other family members about the phone and the ad we had in the paper and how delighted I was with myself. Then the phone rang; it was my first call and I was ecstatic. 'Hello,' I said, 'All Brite Cleaning. How can I help you?' 'Mom,' the voice at the end of the line said, 'will you bring home milk and bread.'

I was mortified, but it didn't end there. I was like a child with a new toy so I went out of the room and said, 'Hang up and ring again but don't say anything'. I wanted to pretend to those in the house that it was a business call. I went back in and the phone rang again. I went through my 'professional voice' spiel but they had copped on to what I was up to and laughed their hearts out. After a somewhat embarrassing start, that mobile phone served me well for the next three years.

Once the ad was in the local paper, I quickly got an office to clean on a weekly basis which was great. We also did any individual houses that we got but, at that time, people weren't into having their homes professionally cleaned like they are now; you would be lucky to get a house-clean if somebody died or some very special event was taking place, but it wasn't the norm to clean a house on a weekly basis. We got work with a couple of builders and in a few hotels, in addition to the cleaning of holiday homes and guesthouses.

Even though the work was building up, the first few years were torture financially. We had to pay insurance every month, as well as the fuel for the van. We took any work we got and were ready to do what it took to get our name out there. During those early years, I became a dab hand at being inventive with all the different types of dinners you could make with mince meat; I would buy the best quality meat I could afford but I've no doubt that the family definitely had an overdose of it eventually!

It is never easy when you are in the start-up phase of a business. Budgeting can be very hard to do effectively. In our early days, we had jobs coming in but most of them were one-offs and we couldn't predict how many would come in during any one week. Getting a few regular clients who were good to pay was what we were after. Outside of the ad I religiously put in *Kerry's Eye*, there was no budget for any other advertising. But the fact that we didn't have a budget meant that other ways of getting our name out there that didn't cost a lot of money had to be found.

It was a really hard learning curve but I was determined to make this cleaning business work. I could see there was a need for a service such as we were offering; the economic recovery was slowly trickling out from the cities to the rural areas and there was a bit more building taking place. Patience was the quality most often needed during our first two or three years; I knew where we wanted to go but it wasn't going to happen overnight and it was going to demand sacrifice and perseverance.

MY MOTHER'S LIFE had never been easy. Since her youth, when her parents and two brothers died of TB, to the death of her brother Donie a decade later, and the difficult life she had with my father, the endless hardship and grief she suffered took its toll on her health. From the time Joan died in 1994, her health started to deteriorate more rapidly. When I returned from London I tried to spend as much time as I could with her. It was very dispiriting, however, to visit her and find that she hadn't got out of bed that day, and to know that depression was getting a firm grip on her mind. She was on a lot of medication for a variety of ailments which were never really examined to try and find the source of the illness. And she was still addicted to cigarettes, a habit she could never break even though she suffered from emphysema.

She didn't create a network for herself and was quite isolated apart from her immediate family, and I could see the negative effect that was having on her mental health. She didn't go out or socialise much and would stay inside most of the time. We all need outlets to release our pent-up emotions and she didn't have any for all that pain she'd had to internalise. Still, she had a great wit and was apt to sing a song the odd time. When she was in good form, she could be great fun but when she was down she wouldn't be able to talk to you at all.

About a year and a half after Joan died, my mother went into hospital and more or less spent the final ten months of her life there. In that time, she improved enough to go to a convalescent home, but she was there for only two weeks before she returned to the General Hospital in Tralee. She was in Loher Ward, nicknamed locally as 'God's Waiting Room'. I visited her every couple of days and the week before she died she asked me to bring her some rhubarb and custard. She had always loved warm rhubarb. I brought it in and fed her some but she ate only a few spoonfuls. The next week she died, on the 17th of September 1996, at the age of seventy-two. We were so sad to lose her but I've no doubt it was a release for her. Her life had never been easy but I always hoped that the love and esteem her children had for her eased her burden somewhat.

FOR ANYONE in business, but especially when you are starting up, cashflow is key. Without it, you can't succeed and it is one of the hardest things to get in place and to keep under control when you are self-employed. When we started All Brite Cleaning Services, we had little or no cashflow. I had a personal bank account in Tralee since before going to London and this was the account we used when we started up. On the day in April 1995 when I registered the name, there was £74 in the account. That is what we had left in the bank account after buying the items we needed—and we kept them to a bare minimum—to start our business. It was hard to manage our cashflow because the people we worked for were often waiting to be paid themselves and sometimes we had to wait and wait.

My biggest fear was not having enough money to pay our bills. I certainly didn't want to start getting into debt again; after our earlier experiences, I was nearly paranoid about it. We were usually paid on a Friday and I would lodge the cheques on the following Monday. There was no online banking at the time so every Monday morning I would go into the bank first thing to check the balance and see what bills we would be able to pay that week. In the first few years, it was always very tight between what was coming in and what had to go out. The only time I could really relax was at the weekend when the banks were closed and nothing could be done. The pressure would be back again on Monday morning and this cycle went on for months and months.

A lovely woman who worked in the bank knew how hard I was working to keep my head above water. She would tell me if our account had come to the bank's attention and would warn me to make sure that there was enough money to pay our debts. At one point in 1997, a payment I was expecting didn't come through. I called into the bank and asked for an overdraft of £200, a facility I hadn't asked for up to that point. I explained that we had a good bit of work lined up; that, in fact, we had work done and payment was now due. But they said no and a cheque I had just written to our cleaning supplies company for £400 bounced.

When I wasn't long in business, I had been told to never let a cheque bounce because your good name could go with it. I was absolutely mortified; for me, it was a first. I explained to the supplies company that I would sort out their payment and they were fine about it. Dealing with the bank, however, was another thing altogether.

After they refused me an overdraft, the woman in the bank rang me on Friday evening. She said she had seen how stressed I was. 'Why don't you pull out of it now and cut your losses?' she said. 'They are thinking of closing your account.' I panicked and my head was all over the place. Would the next cheque bounce? What was going to happen on Monday morning when the bank opened again? I was depending on being paid for the work we had done and if that payment didn't come in on Monday, we were going to be in even more trouble. I was fast learning that we shouldn't have paid out until we had payments in and safely lodged in the bank. Our clients had promised faithfully to pay up but there just wasn't enough money turning up on time for us to meet outward payments.

We were now in a serious dilemma. All that night I thought about the money that was owed to us and if there was any way I could get it in by Monday morning so the next cheque wouldn't bounce. By the time I woke up on Saturday morning, I had made a decision: I wasn't going to lose the business just because the bank didn't want to support us; we were owed money and I was going to get it. There was one client that owed about £1,300 and all we owed the bank was about £200; that money was coming to us and there was no way we were going out of business just because the bank didn't believe in us.

I rang the client and said that I would be calling to them on Sunday to collect the cheque. They were a good, regular customer but you would have to wait two months to get paid. I'd already been following them up for the payment but now I told the manager that I absolutely needed to collect that money. 'I just have to have it by Monday morning,' I said, 'or we'll be out of business.'

I told Seán what I was doing and said I would be back later. I drove to Dingle and the man I was looking for wasn't available; I was told that he was on a break so I sat and waited. There was no way I was going home and coming back again. After an hour, he turned up. He was very understanding but said that while he could sign the cheque, it had to be countersigned and the person who could do that wouldn't be around until the morning. 'I have to have that cheque for tomorrow morning,' I said. 'Can't you go to the person in question and ask him to sign it?'

There were tears in my eyes, I was so desperate and determined. 'I wouldn't have come out all this way to waste your time and my time if I didn't need it.' He made a phone call but the person who needed to countersign the cheque wasn't there. 'Go home,' he said to me, 'and I promise you he will be in at ten in the morning and we will get the second signature then.' 'That's fair enough,' I said. 'I'll be back then.'

My dilemma now was that I had about £2 in my pocket and almost no petrol in the car. I wasn't going home because I couldn't afford to drive back again in the morning. I rang Seán and said there was a delay and I didn't know what time I would be back. At that point, I didn't say that I was going to stay for the night. He knew that I did mad things sometimes but he didn't think I was that cracked. I had the price of a cheese sandwich and a cup of tea which I bought in a cheap café and then I parked up in front of the marina. It was a nice summer's evening and I had nothing better to do than to walk around the town. I did a lot of window shopping and enjoyed the snatches of Irish I could hear when I passed locals. I love the Irish language and to hear it being spoken so fluently was a bright moment in an otherwise dark day.

I couldn't keep walking forever and eventually I got into the car and rang Seán again. I told him that I was collecting the cheque early in the morning so it wasn't worth my while going home. He wasn't too happy with the situation but I assured him that I would be fine. It wasn't an unpleasant night and I eventually fell asleep. When I woke up, just before dawn broke, I looked at the car clock: it was ten to six. I had four more hours to wait. This was the hardest part so I got out of the car and went for a walk.

When I found an open shop with a bathroom I went in and tried to make myself presentable. I wandered around and by twenty past nine I was back in the building, ready to collect my money. The manager was there and expressed surprise at seeing me so early. 'You're back,' he said. 'I am,' I said. 'I told you I would be. I can't go back to Tralee without the money.' About an hour later, the second man turned up and the manager disappeared into an office. When he returned, he handed me a brown envelope containing the cheque. There was no way to describe the relief I felt at that moment.

I got into the car and headed for Tralee. Now my attention went to the fuel gauge: the tank was almost empty. I had a cheque for £1,300 but no cash. On the long road home, I was waiting for the car to stall but, thankfully, whatever petrol was left was enough to bring me back. My first port of call was the bank. I went in, paid them what I owed them and took the rest in cash and went straight across the road to another bank and opened an account there that very morning.

They welcomed me and I lodged about £600, keeping the rest for the family. To celebrate our survival, I went to the Grand Hotel and had breakfast. The friendly woman from the bank where I had just closed my account joined me. I told her that I had thought long and hard about what she had said to me and that when I considered the two years of hard work and sacrifice that we had put into building the foundations of the business, there was no way I was going to let the bank take it away from us. I knew in my heart there was no way I was ever going to let that happen.

ONCE we'd survived that first big challenge to All Brite Cleaning Services, I was more determined than ever to grow the business. A short time later, I was in my friend's shop waiting to be served when I overheard two women talking. One said that the cleaning tender for the Eircom building was up for renewal. I knew what a tender was but I had never had to submit one before. I'm all for asking for what you need so when I left the shop I phoned Eircom and asked for details. I was told that all tenders had to be in by Friday; it was now Wednesday which meant I only had two days to get my tender in and the forms were in Limerick. There was nothing else for it; I got into my car and drove to Limerick. I had never been in that city before but I eventually arrived and found the Eircom office. I met up with the man I had spoken to on the phone. He was surprised to see me but gave me the forms and told me to fill them out and send them back by post.

I took them and decided that I needed to get the tender filled and returned there and then as there was no certainty that it would arrive on time by post. The nearest place I could go was a toy store on the next street so I positioned myself among the aisles of furry animals and set about completing our first tender form. I phoned Seán and together we managed to fill in all the necessary details. Neither of us had a clue how to price the job because we weren't familiar with the building but I knew someone who had worked there as a cleaner so I rang her to see how long she spent there each day. 'Four hours daily,' she said. I wrote down that we would get the work done in three. What I wanted more than anything was to get my foot in the door of this company. Then I ran back to the office and dropped off the tender form.

The following Monday, the man in the Limerick office rang me. He asked me how come our price was so low and how could we possibly get the work done in the time outlined. 'You don't know me and how fast I work,' I replied.

'I'd like to meet you,' he said, 'because if you can do it in that amount of time, you must be Superwoman.' We met up that week and he was one of the nicest men I had ever met. I told him my story, including how I had overheard the women talking about the tender and how I had gone into Toys 'R' Us to complete the form. I said I was really anxious to get more work, especially contract work such as Eircom was offering. 'But you will only have £7 a week out of it,' he said. 'It doesn't sound right, but since you are after driving all the way down, I am going to give it to you.' That was how we won the first tender we ever submitted.

I was excited and terrified in equal measure; we hadn't seen the inside of the building so we had no real idea what we were undertaking. For the first few weeks I cleaned it myself and, working flat out, I was able to get the job done in three hours. Then I got a girl in to do the work; I gave her a hand but there were other jobs I needed to do and I wanted the same person on that contract all the time. A short time later, I got a call from the man in the Limerick office. He asked if we wanted to tender for some more work in Eircom at their Limerick city office, which was four times the size of the one in Tralee.

Seán and I went to inspect the premises and this time round we did the calculations properly and priced the work at a more realistic rate. There wasn't a problem upping the hourly rate for the job and we secured the contract. We had thrown a sprat to catch a salmon and we got a good haul with that sprat because we subsequently got about twenty-two Eircom RSUs (hub stations in rural areas) to clean in the Limerick and Kerry areas. Seán and my brother Danny looked after them. We were with Eircom for about three years when all their cleaning went up for tender again and they decided to get one company to cover the whole country. There was no way we could do that so we bowed out, but we had got a great leg up from them. They were our first big contract, giving us regular work which was what we really needed at the time.

All Brite Cleaning Service's reputation for working hard and delivering on promises meant that work such as initial cleans for builders, supermarkets, schools and contracts such as Eircom were growing. I would happily walk into an office and make a cold call; I just loved that— walking in not knowing what might happen and the buzz of securing new work. I was a great networker and it was more informal in those days. I always had business cards; they were my bible and wherever I went, I would pull one out and give it to somebody because they could know a company that might need our services. I was a great believer in word-of-mouth advertising. We also had a few vans on the road by now and the first thing we did with the vans was put our name and contact details on them; the amount of work we got from people who saw our vans and took down the number was significant.

BY 1999, things were going very well for All Brite Cleaning. Both work and cashflow were looking healthy although getting money in was always a challenge. In spite of our healthy profits, Seán and I had never drawn a wage from the business; we took only what we needed but never gave ourselves regular payment. Then, at a meeting with our accountant, he asked us a question that was like a wake-up call. 'What is the point in working if you are not paying yourself?' he said. 'You have to get into the habit of paying yourself or else you are just working to pay others.' We saw his point. When we came out from that meeting, we both agreed that we would draw a regular wage from then on.

Getting that money every two weeks made a big difference to my attitude. 'This is great,' I said to Seán, 'we are making enough money to pay ourselves now; this feels good.' This simple—though very important—act gave me self-belief and made me want to work harder. Not taking a wage is something most self-employed people have to do for some period of time. Everyone else gets paid and you are last to get paid but you have to pay yourself as soon as it is feasible, otherwise there is no point. I saw very clearly then how important it is to reward yourself to maintain your motivation; to continue going without can break your own self-esteem.

We had been running our office from home but, as the business grew, we rented space in a small room in Tralee town where the rent was low. In early 2000, we moved office to Basin Road, Tralee, where we bought a building. We were making good profits at this stage and, after another chat with our accountant, we decided that buying rather than renting would make sense. We weren't big socialisers or spenders and wanted to see something concrete for all our hard work, and buying a property seemed like a very good idea. Around then I also started thinking that it would be wonderful to be able to give a home to each of our children. There had been a lot of chaos and upheaval in their younger years and I thought if we could give them something back, if we could set each of them up with a roof over their heads, it would go a good way towards making all the sacrifice worthwhile.

GETTING the Eircom contract was a vital turning point for us and from the time we got it we continued to grow and expand. By 2000, we were doing very good business and became a limited company with a new name, ABC Cleaning Services and Supplies. We had fifteen on the payroll and were servicing several contracts, both big and small. We were steadily becoming one of the biggest cleaning companies in the southern part of the country. Most of our children were adults at this point. One of our sons was working full time with us while the others were in college or had jobs. Some of the older boys were now were getting married and having their own children. Our younger children were still in school while the youngest member of the family was eight.

The year 2000 was also significant for Seán and myself because it was the year we went on our first holiday abroad since we had gone to America in 1970. Our children organised and paid for it as they knew we would never get around to organising it ourselves. We went to Portugal for two weeks but, no matter how hard I tried, I just couldn't switch off. I rang the office constantly, checking this and that in the belief that they couldn't survive without me. Even though I hated to say it, I didn't enjoy being away and all I wanted was to get back to work. I was also aware, however, that Seán and the younger children deserved a holiday, just like other families, so, despite the fact that I had no real interest in taking time off, I agreed to go on another trip the following year.

From that time onwards, we took a holiday at least once a year in different countries and I eventually learned the value of taking time off. By nature, I am a worker and prefer to be busy all the time but I have learned that burnout is inevitable if you don't take a break. Travel also expands the mind because we get to see how other people do things and we can learn from them. I eventually learned to stop ringing the office while I was away which has been a great relief to everyone!

CHAPTER SEVEN

FROM BOOM
TO THE BRINK

HAVING a full building from which to run ABC Cleaning was great and we set up spacious, comfortable offices at Basin Road. Because we had so many contracts and it was becoming more and more difficult to find staff, we brought in a number of employees from other countries and used the bedrooms in the upstairs part of the house for staff accommodation. For the next six to eight years, Ireland was in full boom time. The number of workers on our payroll kept increasing and the contracts kept coming in.

We didn't do any paid-for advertising during these years outside of the local paper we had always used because we didn't need to. We got a website in 2000 and we also made sure that our name was on every van we had on the road. The first brand-new van I bought myself was a Berlingo and I made sure our contact details were put on it. I was driving up and down the country on a weekly basis and people passing me on the road would take the number off the van and the phone kept ringing.

Seán looked after the work in the local region, which included offices, schools, bookies and hotels. We had a small bus and he would travel each day to wherever that work was with the necessary number of workers. There was one person in the office managing that and I looked after everything else, including the securing and overseeing of contracts.

We got a lot of work with national and international retailers which had outlets in Kerry and elsewhere in the country; we looked after the cleaning of several of their stores countrywide. If I knew a retail chain was planning to expand in Ireland—it didn't matter where—I would approach them to see if we could get the cleaning. We got contracts from Cork to Donegal and were working in up to thirteen counties at one time, mostly in retail outlets. Once you got one shop and did a good job, others within the chain would contact you. If you got an outlet in a shopping centre, you would have a great chance of getting the other shops in that centre too.

For these contracts, we hired cleaners and supervisors locally and I would check in on the work every few days. I'd sometimes get a call to say that someone hadn't turned up for work and that was a nightmare. It was not a problem if someone didn't turn up where there were several people on a job, but if there was only one and they didn't show, then we were in trouble. I often had to travel up the country in the morning and bring staff with me to cover a contract because a cleaner hadn't shown up, and that was very difficult. I developed a policy of having at least two people on every job as a no-show is unacceptable in our business.

Some of the shops had twenty-four-hour opening and

they would have to be cleaned in the early morning as cleaners are, generally, expected to be gone by the time everyone else comes to work. I would normally start at five in the morning and could be going all day long until seven or eight o'clock at night. I had to manage cleaning staff at either end of the day, as well as getting new contracts during the day. I was once working on a contract near Dublin and was on the way home to Kerry after the day's work when I got a call about another potential contract in that area; I had nothing to do but turn the car. If we didn't strike while the iron was hot, we wouldn't get the job.

We would clean on a Saturday night rather than a Sunday morning to give the cleaners a day off. It was very important that the staff got time off so we would ask for a night clean, which was anytime after nine o'clock. I liked Saturday nights after work was done, and looked forward to the very welcome rest that Sundays offered.

TRAVELLING around the country was very tough and I often slept in the van overnight. In 2005, because I was travelling so much, I decided that I needed a good, decent car. Someone advised me to get a Mercedes because they were safe, solid and comfortable. I didn't smoke and rarely drank so I felt I was, finally, entitled to this luxury for myself. Things were going extremely well at ABC and the company bank account looked very healthy. We were about to go on holiday and I called into the bank the day before we headed off to Turkey and explained that I needed a loan of €30,000 to buy a company car.

The next day, when Seán and I were lying on a Turkish beach, my phone rang. It was the bank telling me that the loan had been approved and the money was in our account. 'Can you believe it?' I said in shock. 'There is €30,000 in our bank account! What will we do with it?' In answer to my own question, I said, 'I know—we'll buy a property here'. The idea seemed to come out of nowhere. I had never thought of it before but buying a place in Gumbet struck me as a good investment. We loved Turkey very much and always went to the same village where we got to know the people and their culture. I said that I would look around to see if I could find somewhere suitable. A short time later, I came across a property up a hill with a view to die for; it was a traditional Turkish house looking straight onto the ocean and within walking distance of the beach. Before our two-week holiday was over, the sale was completed and the money paid over.

We were definitely bitten by the property bug because, again in 2005, we sold our property in Basin Road and bought a bigger one in Boherbee as we needed more office space. We also bought an apartment in Limerick city centre and another house in Tralee which we rented. We then bought the cottage from my Uncle Johnny and demolished it and built a new house on the site. We borrowed for that project and, again, there was no problem getting money from the bank.

The dream I had of buying a property to give to each of our eight children was fast becoming a reality. On paper, I was the proud owner of six properties. From the time we had started building the business, I had wanted to give them something that I hadn't had. It was hard to build up the business and they would have preferred if they had seen more of me at home but at least if I could give them something to start their own lives, it would make up in some way for my absence in their youth. I had it 100 per cent in my mind to buy eight properties, one for each son and daughter, and I worked around the clock to try and achieve that.

By the start of 2007, ABC Cleaning was employing approximately 350 people. Outside the main urban areas, we were now the biggest rural-based cleaning company in the country. We were growing so quickly that we were coming into competition with some of the main contract-cleaning names in Ireland, companies that had been in existence for decades. We had a huge number of contracts in 2007 and the business looked very healthy on paper. Turnover was large and we were working around the clock. Rumours of a recession were starting to spread, however, and people were saying that the boom was coming to an end. Any worries we had were eased by the government which reassured everyone with talk of a soft landing.

We were in expansion mode all the time and didn't have the time—or take the time—to stand back and look at the bigger picture. In the late noughties, we didn't have the company infrastructure in place that we have today. There was just one girl in the office and she was trying to manage all office-related work. We didn't have a dedicated accounts section or a dedicated HR department, nor did we have comprehensive health and safety procedures. I was trying to be all things to all people and ended up being a jack-of-all-trades. When you do that, you will inevitably fall on your knees. I was like a hamster in a wildly spinning wheel. When you first set up your business, you try and do everything yourself. That works for a little while but when the business expands, you need to step back and say, 'I need support, I need a team, I need help; we need a person for accounts, for marketing, for HR'. However, I didn't do that.

Additionally, I was still pricing some jobs low in order to get them. We would do a spreadsheet and it would look fine on paper but, if anything went wrong, we were in trouble because we hadn't factored in such eventualities, or looked at the impact things going wrong would have—such as if a machine broke down and we had to pay someone to fix it. I didn't look at costs as closely as I should have. I wanted the quantity and the quality, but for the quantity we had and the quality of work we put in, we were not getting the return.

While we had a big turnover and a lot of staff, our profits were going down. Our biggest profit margin had been in 2002 but from 2003 onwards, as the company got bigger and bigger, our profit margin became tighter and tighter. In addition to that, there was one client—our largest—whose practices were leading us into waters where we were increasingly out of our depth.

ABOUT seven years earlier, I had secured work locally with one of Ireland's largest retail companies. I was thrilled with myself and within a short space of time we had another one of their outlets on our books as well. I had secured the initial job in the manner I had honed and polished over the years: I walked into the local store and asked to talk with the manager. 'Who do I contact if I want to get the cleaning contract here?' I asked. He gave me the name of someone in the Dublin office. I rang and asked for a meeting, saying, 'I'd like to tell you what I do and how I can help you'. I'll remember those words for the rest of my life; I don't know where they came from.

We made an appointment and I went to Dublin for the meeting. I outlined why he should consider giving ABC Cleaning a trial and, by the time I was on the road home, I had secured the store in Tralee; I was ecstatic. We ended up getting the cleaning contract for twenty-two of their stores in different areas in the country, and they nearly broke us.

From the time we got the first store, we increased the number of outlets from that group at a rate of approximately three per year. They were all in different places and I set up teams around the country for each outlet we serviced. By 2007, we had taken on 150 staff just to cover the cleaning work with this giant retailer. But the rate at which we were expanding was making me uneasy; I didn't feel in control of things anymore. I knew that we weren't making a profit from our work with this group. With the amount of time, effort, machinery and the number of products the work demanded, and for the pay we were getting, the sums just weren't adding up.

Then, in 2007, the company put the cleaning of their stores up for tender using an online bidding system. Contract cleaning companies were invited to bid live online for various stores. If we wanted to hold onto the stores we had, we had no option but to put in our bids. We soon saw that, instead of going up, per-hour cleaning rates were coming down at an alarming rate. The lowest rate I believed could be charged per hour per store was €14 but the price kept dropping. We had to decide if we wanted to hold onto the stores or not. We could see the numbers coming up on the screen but we didn't know who was bidding against us as it was a blind system. I remember saying at one stage that if the hourly rate went below a certain amount we couldn't take it. We made the decision to pull out when we had dropped our hourly rate to €11.

As far as I was concerned, we had left the bidding and had lost the stores. The next day, however, someone from head office got in touch with me and said we had secured the work for €11 per hour. Basically, they had managed to bring us down from €14 to €11 per hour, undercutting ourselves without ever knowing if there was any other bidder. I got very nervous when that happened. Once they had cut the hourly rate, they also reduced the time in which we had to complete the work. It felt as if we had been sucked into something over which we had no control. We had no actual contract with the retailer, just non-binding agreements that gave us no security.

BECAUSE this client's work was priced so low, our other contracts were, effectively, subsidising the work we were doing for this large contract. Added to that was the problem of late payments. Everyone was paying later because they weren't getting paid on time themselves and didn't have the cashflow they needed; we were all in the same position. The big wheel continued turning but it was going slower and slower. Even though there was still a lot of money around the economy generally, late payments were becoming more common and they were having a significant impact on cashflow. With most clients, when I rang and explained that we really needed them to make their payment, we usually got the money eventually. With the large retailer, however, that wasn't the case. They were tough and held out as long as they wanted.

The norm with our contracts was that we had to wait two full months before receiving payment. During that time, staff wages, tax, insurance and all other bills still had to be paid. With late payments added in, this was a very long time to be left waiting for money to come into our account to meet all our outgoings. As our cashflow problems became more evident, I spoke to our accountant who told me about invoice discounting. This system gives you access to cash when you have cashflow problems. The accountant advised me to apply for it which I did.

In this system, you give the bank a copy of the invoice and they give you 70 per cent of its value up front. When it is paid, the client's payment goes directly to the invoice discounting account in the bank. Essentially, it is a loan for a short period of time and the bank specifies the period of time by which they are to be repaid. The system works well if you are getting paid regularly but, if payment is late, the charges and penalties incurred are very high.

We were so strapped for cash that I'd be waiting for the end of the month to arrive so that I could hand the invoice copy to the bank and get the 70 per cent payment. But with late payments, our penalties were growing exponentially. The giant retailer, in particular, could let payment go overdue by three months or longer and then, by the time payment was made, it was all swallowed up in charges and penalties payable to the bank under the invoice discounting system. What we were paying in penalties was nearly the same as the value of the invoice itself. We were making nothing over the fourteen months we were involved in this system.

Then the bank stopped allowing us avail of the system because the payments just weren't coming in on time. Additionally, there wasn't enough money coming into our main bank account, so we had two banks down on top of us. There was no money to pay the big bills and we owed a huge amount to Revenue. If we had been paid by everyone we were working for, including the large retailer, we still wouldn't have been able to pay everyone because the large retailer was sucking the life blood from all our other contracts: we had become unviable.

By late 2007, the perfect storm finally broke. Revenue contacted our bank to stop all outward payments; the bank where we were doing the invoice discounting pulled the plug on that facility, and our main bank put a stop on our company account. ABC Cleaning was heading towards insolvency. The figures weren't stacking up and it seemed that everything, literally, was gone. I knew things had been going steadily downhill for several months but I kept going until the last hour, hoping we would be paid and that, somehow, the books would balance. I wanted desperately to keep going, at least until Christmas, even though I couldn't see how we could continue after that. I was under so much pressure. There was money going out at every hand's turn and nowhere near enough coming in.

AT THE END of that year, we were owed a very large payment by the large retailer. It was coming up to Christmas and I had to pay the staff. You could be a day or two late with wages at other times of the year but not at Christmas. We paid once a month and when there was sufficient money in the account, I would always pay staff a day or two early. I was due to pay them on the 1st of December and this retailer didn't give a flying fiddlers. I contacted them and said I had to have the money they owed because I had to pay our staff. 'You'll have it,' they replied. Still it didn't appear.

I contacted them again and said my son would travel to Dublin to collect the cheque. They said fine; he could come up and personally collect it. The next morning, I dropped him to the airport at Farranfore to get the early flight. On my way back I called into the post office; to my surprise, there was the cheque from the retailer for me which had been posted on the same day they had told me they would keep it for my son to collect.

Even with the payment from them, we were still short a significant amount for the wages. One of the staff said that she had €3,000 in savings and would give that to me to help make up the shortfall. I had some savings in the credit union but we were still short. The wages were paid by direct transfer into employees' accounts and if there was any shortfall in our account, no payment at all would be made. We had done everything possible to put as much as we could together but we still didn't have enough. More in hope than anything else, we pressed the button to make the payment.

I cried in the office with two or three of the staff who were there and told them that I didn't think we would be opening after Christmas. I asked them not to say anything to the other workers for the moment. Then I went home and for the first time in my life I went to bed and buried my head under the blankets, waiting for the explosion to happen when the staff realised that they hadn't been paid.

The following morning, at about ten past eight, my phone rang. I was still in bed which was most unusual for me as I was normally always up before dawn. It was the girl who had given her €3,000 savings. 'You won't believe it,' she said, 'but my wages are in my account.' I jumped out of bed, delighted; at least the staff had been paid. For some unknown reason, the money had gone through.

Around noon, I got a call from the bank. They said that the money shouldn't have gone through because there was a stop on my account and there hadn't been enough money to pay the full wages. Whatever system they had in place, the message hadn't been communicated from Tralee to

Dublin quickly enough and when the button was pressed, the payment had been authorised. Once that happened it couldn't be reversed. I said there was nothing I could do about the fact that the payment had gone through. This was the 22nd of December and we would be closed over Christmas and not due to re-open until the 4th of January. The staff were paid until the 1st of January so I had a bit of breathing space. We were in a crisis situation yet I couldn't accept that all was lost; there had to be a way out of this, I believed, it just couldn't be the end.

IT WAS HARD to get into the festive spirit. I thought if I could get over Christmas Day without breaking down, if I could make some attempt to enjoy it and be happy for the sake of the family, that was as much as I could hope to achieve. The 25th and 26th passed in a blur of people and food and the busyness that is usual in our home at that time of the year. By the 27th, however, I felt the sharp pain in my stomach that reminded me—even though I didn't need any reminder—that time was passing and I had to take action.

I had a very good friend who had always been incredibly good to me and whose advice I really respected. I rang her and we arranged to meet up. I told her the full story; in fact, she was the first person to hear in its entirety what had been going on over the past few years. She asked if I minded if she spoke to a businessman whom she knew and admired. I was happy to agree. The next day she rang and said she had set up a meeting for me with a man named

Peter who was working as a consultant. He was very well connected in business circles, she said, and might know of someone who would invest in ABC Cleaning.

I knew Peter by reputation as a very good guy. As the accountant's office was still closed due to the holidays, my son Liam prepared figures for the meeting he and I had with Peter. The most up-to-date accounts available, from the year 2006–2007, did not look good at all. The spreadsheet detailing what we were paying out and what was coming in—laid out in black and white—including all the crippling invoice discounting costs, was shocking to see.

I wasn't holding out for any miracles but Peter said he would talk to someone he knew who might be interested in investing. He had done business with this man on several occasions and, while there were no guarantees, he said he would try his best. It was a relief to know there was someone on our side. He got in touch a few times over the next few days looking for additional information. On the 5th of January, he rang and said he had an investor who was interested in the company. The potential investor wanted to see the full accounts, which I couldn't get until a couple of days later when the accountant's office re-opened.

When he finally got to go through the accounts, the investor told Peter he thought there was a future in the company. He made an offer: he would invest €158,000 for a 51 per cent stake in ABC Cleaning, leaving us with 49 per cent. I was delighted and gutted at the same time. I had lost control of the company but a voice in my head was telling me that half a loaf was better than no loaf.

There was a lot of toing and froing over the next few weeks and the contract was finally signed on the 25th of January 2008. We had survived.

THERE WERE changes straightaway. Peter took a hands-on role in the running of the company which was great because there were hard cuts coming down the line. In a small, family-run business it is difficult to tell staff—people you know well and personally—that their wages are going to be cut, so it made it easier that Peter would do that instead of me. Staff wages were significantly reduced across the board. The way I saw it, I couldn't ask them to take such a cut and not take it myself so both Seán and I took the same cut as the staff in our wages. Since I had started in business, I had been paying a small monthly amount to a charity and that was stopped, things were that tight. We had to close off all the rooms in the building where we had our offices and move into one small room to cut down on the cost of electricity and heating; everything was cut back to the bare bones.

As 2008 progressed, every contract was examined individually to see how the figures were stacking up. Then, in April, the giant retailer gave notice that its online bidding for cleaning contracts was again taking place; if we wanted to hold on to their stores, we would have to bid for the work. Peter, Liam and I put in our bids and we secured the stores again. With a more streamlined company, we hoped that we could make it work but, by September 2008, we realised we had no option but to give up working with this company.

From April to September, we did a full audit of what it was worth to us to have them as a client, which was not easy as they would not sign a contract and were liable to change the hours and nature of the work being done on what seemed like a whim. We saw clearly that we weren't making any money from them and couldn't make money by having them on our books. We had to let them go. This was a big decision as there was a certain kudos in having such a large client on our books. Also, having them made us look like a much bigger company with a large turnover and number of employees, making it easier for us to get other big contracts.

I wrote to them and said it was no longer viable for ABC Cleaning to do business with them. I said we were going to downsize and keep business local instead of travelling around the country. We wouldn't let them stuck, I added, and would stay with them for two months until they found someone else. They asked if we wanted to keep the local stores but I said no, we needed to make a clean break. Once they were gone, ABC Cleaning looked much smaller; over a period of fourteen months we had come down to about sixty staff from a peak of nearly 350.

In November of that year, our luck turned and we secured the IT Tralee (ITT) cleaning contract. We had put in our tender months earlier; it was our first time going for such a big contract and the specifics of such tendering processes were new to me. My son Liam and I did a three-day course on 'How to submit a winning tender' in Dublin before filling out the tender form. The course cost a lot of money but it was worth every penny. It was like manna from heaven to secure this work and it was a huge boost to the company. We now had a very big contract on our own doorstep and that was a real blessing.

The work had to be done in the early mornings and in the evenings and, if there were events on, we would have to cover them too. It wasn't the be-all and end-all of everything but it was a good chunk of what was keeping the company afloat. It was great to know that, unless we did something drastic altogether, we were not going to lose the contract—and we had no notion of losing it; we had every intention of giving it our best shot.

Under the previous contractor, the cleaning staff at the college had been paid once a fortnight. When we took over we told them that payment would be once a month. We were still experiencing cashflow problems at the time and, as the ITT was paying us once a month, it would be impossible for us to pay staff for work that we hadn't yet been paid for. The last thing I wanted in this new and very important contract was to not be able to pay the wages so we had to get the cleaning staff to move to monthly payments. We had to negotiate this through the workers' union and, in the end, agreement was reached. A few of the staff who were near retirement age left but most stayed on and the contract went very well.

WE WERE well into the process of downsizing and streamlining when the recession hit hard. In a way, we were lucky because we were already in survival training mode. By the time the full force of the economic downturn was felt, I knew how lucky we had been to leave the giant retailer as they cut rates at will during that time. We would have gone to the wall if we had still been with them. As it was, most of the UK and national Irish retailers put all their contracts up for tender from 2008 onwards.

The penny had dropped with everybody in business that the recession was biting and so they went to the market to see what they could get. We lost some of the national contracts we had because they went nationwide. There was no way we could even think about going for anything nationally now because the money wasn't there, full stop; there was no way we could consider expansion at this time.

We were lucky to hold on to our local contracts, including a cross-section of offices, schools and a few hotels that we had contracts with between 2007 and 2009. We had about fifteen staff a day servicing these hotels. We never spread our wings too far with this type of work because one day you would get a phone call saying, 'We have fifty occupancies and need five staff over' and the day after it might be a different number so you never knew where you were with them. Finally, after about two years, I decided that we would move away from servicing hotels and concentrate on the contract cleaning.

WHILE THE SHIP was being steadied and I could see light on the horizon, our investor wasn't so happy. He had come into ABC Cleaning with the intention of making a return on his investment but, unfortunately, we were still in troubled waters. I had to make a deal. We had been decreasing our losses steadily over the previous three years but we still weren't making significant profits. Business was improving but it wasn't enough; I went to Peter and asked his advice. 'We'll offer him a monthly payment until his investment is paid off,' he said. That was the only option we had to ensure our survival.

We prepared a proposal to which the investor agreed. It included the legally binding caveat that, if a payment was missed, he would become the sole owner of the company. I had to take another pay cut but, strangely, the fact that the investor was exiting took pressure off me. I was very grateful to him for the lifeline he had thrown us; if it wasn't for him we would have had no business at all. From January 2011, we made the payments until we eventually paid off the full investment in January 2014.

The cutbacks had to continue and we were quickly in the same boat as so many others who had invested in property during the noughties. We got rid of the house in Turkey, the apartment in Limerick and the house in Tralee as soon as we could. Their value had dropped stratospherically but we couldn't keep them. We still had the building in Boherbee where our office was. In 2012, we turned the upstairs rooms into hostel accommodation to try and generate more income but it wasn't anywhere near enough and we didn't have the time to focus on developing that business while we were trying to consolidate the cleaning business.

We had been paying interest-only on the building in Boherbee and the bank was putting pressure on us to pay them back for the property. They said they couldn't understand why we were paying the investor before we paid them. I explained that, without the investor, we didn't have a business and wouldn't be able to pay anyone anything at all. They didn't see that; they wanted their money first. We also owed €75,000 on a loan with our other bank. With the money we had to pay the investor, however, I knew there was no way we could also pay the bank for the property in Boherbee.

We had to make a choice: give back the property or hold onto the business. It wasn't an easy decision and it took me three years to make up my mind. I got a financial specialist in to help us try and solve the issue, or to come to some agreement. But the bank was having none of it and, in July 2015, I handed them the keys of the building in Boherbee. It took me a long time to walk away from that property. I'm a person that doesn't give up easily and I tried everything to try and hold onto it.

Within a year, the building was locked up and put on the market for €180,000; we had paid €450,000 for it. I was very angry with the bank for not being more open to agreement. During the three years that I fought to hold onto the building in Boherbee, I learned more than I had learned in my lifetime before that about dealing with banks, with people who were genuinely trying to help you, and with those who didn't want to help you. It truly was an eye opener.

We moved to an office in Manor West Retail Park for a few months but it wasn't suitable and at the end of 2015 we moved our offices out to Farmers' Bridge, where we had started the company over twenty years earlier in our home. We stayed in the house for a short time until our prefab offices were completed on a site a stone's throw from the front door. Our dream of buying a house for each of the children was now in ashes but we had managed to keep the roof over our heads, something for which I am very grateful.

CHAPTER EIGHT

A NEW PERSPECTIVE

I KNEW in May 2014 that the recession was coming to an end when the phone started ringing more regularly again. One day we got nine phone calls before lunchtime and I knew then that things were changing for the better. At the peak of the boom, around 2007, we would have been getting approximately thirty calls a day. At our lowest ebb, there was a day in 2008 when the phone only rang twice in one day. In 2014, however, I noticed a general change in the mood of people. A recession not only hits our pockets, it also hits our mindsets and we go into recession-think, but I could see that people were again looking at getting their homes cleaned for Holy Communions and confirmations and were feeling more confident overall.

We had eighty-nine on the payroll and there had been year-on-year growth for the previous few years. The upward trajectory was small, but it was going in the right direction and we were on a solid foundation. We had a very good local business with a healthy number of solid clients. We were lucky that we had managed to hold on to most our local business throughout the recession.

Our son Brian worked with us for a year around this time and he was brilliant at marketing; he was full of new ideas and energy and really brought us up to date when it came to connecting with customers. He oversaw new developments, such as sending out brochures, asking for feedback and getting involved in corporate social responsibility. Having come through two recessions, I didn't want to spend much but he helped me overcome my innate reluctance to spend on marketing. He also got a good number of new contracts for us thanks, in no small part, to his genuinely warm personality and great way of dealing with people.

I also took his advice about getting more staff to deal with certain areas of the business. I was still wearing too many hats and finally accepted that if we were to continue consolidating and expanding, there was no way I could do it all myself, as I had done in the past. We got a dedicated accounts person and now we know at the press of a button what our cashflow is; there is no hiding from the fact of what our bottom line is and that honesty with ourselves is very liberating. Our health and safety is outsourced to Sheila Nolan, one of the best people working in this area in the country. For many years, we couldn't afford a HR person but now I know we can't afford not to have one. In 2016, we availed of the services of the HR Suite and they take care of all our HR issues. This has freed me and other office staff up greatly so we can focus on other work.

We also hired a dedicated sales and marketing manager who has taken over from me and is now making the links and finding new clients and contracts. He goes out and knocks on doors, hands in his card politely and asks if he can make an appointment. He makes sure that we have our figures done before we give a price. Everything is dissected, from A to Z, before we put in a price. We have really turned around how we operate in comparison with the time when we just wanted to get more work.

When we negotiate contracts, we send prospective clients our company profile, including a list of who we work for, and they can read the testimonials which we put up with the permission of our existing clients who are also happy to give references. That is how confident we are; if we couldn't do that, then we wouldn't go looking for contracts. How you approach people makes all the difference. It is vital for us to keep face-to-face contact with our clients. That means you have to look the part and to always bear in mind that when you go looking for a contract, you can't make demands immediately. You build up to it. I always ask, 'How can I help you?'. You might want to say 'Give it to us' but you can't do that.

We know our product is good; we are not the cheapest and we are not the dearest, but, in my opinion, we are certainly the best. When I first started, I threw a sprat to catch a salmon but the truth is that pricing low will not allow you survive in the long term. Our focus now is on quality and service. We have clients who tell us that they won't go to the market again because they are so happy with us and what we do for them.

Much of our success now is due to our contracts manager, Mairead, our daughter. She came to work with us in 2002 and has become a linchpin in the company, bringing a new approach and expertise to managing contracts. We have never lost a contract that she has managed and we have received many emails from clients saying how delighted they are with how she handles their contract and the level of service she provides. Mairead's motto is, 'Go to the client before they come to you'. If you look after your clients, and keep the lines of communication open and healthy, then you minimise the chance of problems arising, and you also have an excellent basis for solving them when they do.

We still have one contract that I got about thirteen years ago in Tipperary. Mairead has taken over the running of it and she goes up there religiously once a fortnight. She checks the work from top to bottom, meets with the managers and asks for their feedback. It's the same with contracts in Limerick, Cork and elsewhere. This has always been our unique selling point and Mairead has taken it to new levels. We have a very hands-on, close relationship with clients where we invite them to look at the work we have done and to let us know if their needs are being met.

Since Seán retired in 2016, Mairead has become a company director. She is so professional in everything she does, going above and beyond the call of duty, way beyond what I would have dreamed of doing. Working with family in a business can be difficult but the pluses far outweigh the minuses and this is absolutely the case when it comes to Mairead.

THE RULES of business may change over time but the importance of cashflow never will. We look at our cashflow first thing every single morning; in fact, we could be described as cashflow vigilantes. Our approach now is that every single contract has to be dissected to see how viable it is, to assess if it will help grow the business or if it is a Trojan horse that might damage us. We examine it, not only for what it offers and demands in and of itself, but also for how it might impact on the overall company and other contracts. Before, I was just delighted to get new contracts, I wasn't looking at the bigger picture, but that has all changed.

Years ago, we didn't focus enough on pricing, on the hours we had to put in, the cost of the job to us, or its impact on our other contracts. But when the figures don't add up, you can end up working for nothing. The key to solving this is to have a spreadsheet that is a true and accurate reflection of all outgoings and incomings. Regular payment is vital as is having an efficient method of dealing with late payments. We have learned the hard way not to over-price or over-expand.

We are also controlling our cashflow by being careful about the amount of product we buy at any one time and we don't stockpile. I was fortunate many years ago to make contact with a company in Cork. The owner was very tough but she was also very fair. If I asked for credit, she would give me the thirty-one days and say, 'Once you pay by the last day there won't be a problem'. That was twenty-one years ago and I am still with that company. I only deal with two or three suppliers because I like to develop a personal relationship with them. Then it is more likely that they will be good to us in tough times. The payback is that we stick with them as long as we are happy with their products.

We don't lease machines anymore; we buy them instead. We have two professional machines for cleaning carpets and upholstery and we use them almost every day. When we get contracts, we are responsible for supplying all the products and machinery unless there happens to be a machine on site that we can use. We use our own cleaning products unless specifically asked not to if, for example, there is an issue with allergies. We have a small storage area beside our offices where we keep just enough product to service a week's work.

HAVING good contracts is wonderful but having good staff is even better. I have always believed that you should try and do your best for the people that are good to you because, without a good team, you are going nowhere. It is important to get the right staff and to put people in the right positions. Now we have 120 staff, including some who have been with us for over eighteen years. Throughout my time in business, anytime I could reward the staff, I would. We went on days out and for meals with a free bar in hotels in the good times and when we couldn't afford that, I would throw a party in our house. We regularly present awards to staff for service and loyalty.

I strongly believe that we need to recognise people's contribution in work and in life and to reward it, to say

'Thank you' and to honour their achievements. When I was growing up, those closest to me were never able to say 'Well done, Breeda'. I missed that recognition of the value of my contribution. For me it is very important to say to people that their work is valued and respected, and to mean it. It is important to mark milestones and acknowledge the effort made by all. This isn't an easy thing to do and it takes time and commitment to learn how to praise staff.

It also takes time to learn how to be constructively critical. I would always have been seen as the 'bad cop' while Seán was the 'good cop'. I was always the one to tell the staff if something was wrong. I was the tough one, and there were times over the years when I had to be very, very tough. I learned, however, that I needed to mellow and cut people some slack. As we have moved into a stronger position as a company, and as I have learned more about best practice in the workplace, I have managed to do this. I now know that everybody has a different value to the company whereas before I would have thought that they all had to have the same approach and work ethic as me.

I have also learned that everyone has off days. That said, if someone comes into the office in the morning and they have a bad attitude, it doesn't matter who it is (and I know I was the worst myself when things were bad), my belief is they should leave the negative attitude outside the door and not bring it into the office because it can bring everybody down. I tell the staff to remind me of this unwritten rule so that if I am the one coming in with a bad attitude, I, too, need to be told to leave it outside. I like to let them know they can communicate with me in this way.

Of course, good payment is also crucial for keeping staff happy and motivated. As ABC's business improved and we grew more confident that the growth was real, we started the process of reversing wage cuts. As our consolidation and growth persist, we will continue to negotiate new wage agreements with office staff. As members of the Irish Contract Cleaners Association, we comply with wage rates as set out by the Joint Labour Commission for our cleaning personnel.

THROUGH the good times and the bad times I have always been an avid networker. From my earliest days, I handed out our business card with great ease. I have always been a firm believer in the power of word of mouth; it's the best possible advertising so it's important not only that we do good work but also that we are approachable and easy to communicate with.

I got involved in formal networking around 2002 when I started attending Business Network Ireland meetings in Killarney on Thursday mornings. There were usually about seventeen or so people in attendance and it was a very structured forum with an early breakfast meeting— starting at 6.45am and ending at 8.30am. In these groups there can only be one person representing any individual profession so, for example, there wouldn't be two cleaning contractors in any one group.

The aim of the network is that members give each other support by providing real business opportunities. The assumption is that we all know people who might want to avail of members' services, and members make those links and pass on contact details. The network's motto is 'Givers gain'. I went to those meetings regularly for over three years before switching to the Tralee meeting of the same networking group.

I was also involved with a group called BULLET which started with about four people in Tralee, also in 2002. This was a much more informal group; we used rent a room in a hotel and meet in the evening around seven o'clock. The group grew to about ten or so members. BULLET was about meeting up, sharing our business experiences and talking about what we could do better. That group eventually dissolved but out of it grew the Kerry Businesswomen's Network (KBN) in the mid 2000s and I also joined that group.

KBN runs excellent training and networking days and is a very comprehensive support group. Members meet once a month throughout the year. It's good sharing with like-minded people and learning from them. Whereas in my earlier years in business I networked to gain more business, I am now networking to share, to give back and to learn more about speaking in public. Of course, I would never say no to a good cleaning contract!

NETWORKING and creating links with other business-people is great but it's even better when you are recognised as a leader in your area. I was thrilled in 2014 when we were awarded IBEC's Irish Contract Cleaning Association Industry Award for the Best Cleaned Premises Cleaned by a Small Company, sponsored by Diversey Care, for the ITT. Mairead won Supervisor of the Year for the ITT contract at the same awards. Then, in April 2016, I received a lifetime achievement award from Connect Kerry Women in Business Awards.

We celebrated twenty-one years in business that year so it was perfect timing. That was worth more than any money. I always thought money was important because you can't live without it but winning that award meant more to me. Knowing that the hard work and years of sacrifice and struggle are recognised by my peers was huge for me.

When I went to the Connect awards night, I didn't know I was going to win anything although I was really hoping that ABC Cleaning would get an award because it was our twenty-first year in business. As the night went on and prizes were being given out, my face was getting redder and redder with disappointment. Then, at the very end, my name was called out and I jumped out of my seat. I was delighted. I hadn't won anything since getting a book as a prize in national school and this award was the final piece of the jigsaw for me; everything was now in place.

TWENTY-ONE YEARS after setting up the business, having survived two recessions and the many learning curves that being in business bring, ABC Cleaning is now in a very good place and we are optimistic for the future.

We have a solid foundation and our planning is a lot more strategic. We want quantity, but quality is key. I still check the cashflow every morning but we are lucky that we owe very little; that is fantastic and vital to keeping our costs down. We have learned valuable lessons about not buying too much or leasing too many machines, and about keeping transparent and tight control of money coming in and going out.

We have contracts with a variety of sectors including education, medical, pharmaceutical, retail, private and public enterprises, government building and factories. Geographically, we currently work in Kerry, Limerick, Cork, Galway and Tipperary, with plans to strategically expand around the country. Dublin is a huge market and we are looking at it but we are in no rush. We will plan and observe and make our move when we are ready. It's all about planning, goals and milestones. We set goals and make plans around those goals and work towards reaching all the milestones along the route to the big goals.

Mairead has plans to expand the supply part of our business beyond our existing clients. This development means that, not only will we be able to give more value to our existing customers, but we will also reach out new clients who might, in turn, use our cleaning services. Communication is key to developing this side of the business. We listen to what our customers are asking for and respond by meeting those needs. However, any expansion will be done at a steady pace and only when all the foundations are in place.

I AM very happy with where ABC Cleaning is right now; after twenty-one years in business, I can get out of bed, dress up, go into town and be very proud of what we have endured to stay in business and secure a healthy future. I have loved the buzz; even in the hardest of times, when we got a contract—no matter how small—I never lost my passion for making a deal. Nonetheless, I am ready to accept that my work at ABC Cleaning is done. I'll still keep an eye on things and I'll still want reports every Friday, but I am ready to move on. I've given it all I have and now I want to explore other areas that I've long had an interest in.

I want to get back to networking, which I've always loved, but this time I'll be doing it for the love of sharing my story—learned over a lifetime—of trial and error, of failure and success, of always being ready to begin again. I want to encourage people to not give up—to move on to something else if necessary but to never give up. I never once gave up, no matter what obstacles I came across, and there were many. The more times I was pulled down and trod upon, the more determined I was to get up and keep going. I want to encourage people to believe in themselves and to keep trying. I learned the hard way what it is to make mistakes and to fail, but I also know what it is to succeed, and if you give up you will definitely never succeed.

I HAVE some regrets, too. I regret working so hard and not being there for my children as much as I should have been; that is time I will never get back. I remember a Christmas Eve long ago when the house was in chaos and I was trying to get everything ready for the big day. The children were waiting to be fed and I looked around and said, 'Will they ever grow up?'. In what feels like the blink of an eye, they had become adults, doing their own thing. If I had that time back again, I wouldn't worry about the state of the house and would just enjoy having the children around me.

In such a busy life, hurt has occurred along the way. A motto that I fall back on regularly is the Serenity Prayer, especially for some of the personal pain that I carry around unresolved family issues. In life there are always things that happen that we wish hadn't happened and that we dearly wish to change but cannot, or, at least, not at this time. I say the Serenity Prayer to help me maintain hope: *God grant me the serenity to accept the things I cannot change; courage to change the things I can; and wisdom to know the difference.*

Seán is now retired and our children are all living their own lives. All of them have contributed in invaluable ways to helping us build, maintain, consolidate and expand the family business. Our sons Pat and Seánie came on board in the very early days when we came back to Ireland and their contribution was crucial. Brian, Martin, Conor and Ciara have also played vital roles in supporting the business over the years. Liam works in the company while Mairead is steering ABC Cleaning to a bright future.

We have fourteen beautiful grandchildren that are the light of my life. I saw very little of them for a long time due to work and the most important thing for me now is to spend as much time as possible with these wonderful young people. Seán and I like nothing more than having the family come to visit. We have an open-door policy; they come in and out as they wish and we love that.

Now, at the age of sixty-six and receiving my State pension, I—like my grandmother before me—like to put on my finery before heading into town. Instead of using crepe paper to add colour to my cheeks, I am grateful to be able to afford many comforts in life, including make-up. Although I had a harsh childhood and upbringing, I learned early the skills that have enabled me to survive and thrive. After the ups and downs of almost fifty years of marriage, raising a family of eight and charting ABC Cleaning through the stormy seas of business, I am delighted to be in a place of contentment and great hope for more new beginnings.